ANTHONY DE MELLO

MODERN SPIRITUAL MASTERS
Robert Ellsberg, Series Editor

This series introduces the writing and vision of some of the great spiritual masters of the twentieth century. Along with selections from their writings, each volume includes a comprehensive introduction, presenting the author's life and writings in context and drawing attention to points of special relevance to contemporary spirituality.

Some of these authors found a wide audience in their lifetimes. In other cases recognition has come long after their deaths. Some are rooted in long-established traditions of spirituality. Others charted new, untested paths. In each case, however, the authors in this series have engaged in a spiritual journey shaped by the influences and concerns of our age. Such concerns include the challenges of modern science, religious pluralism, secularism, and the quest for social justice.

At the dawn of a new millennium this series commends these modern spiritual masters, along with the saints and witnesses of previous centuries, as guides and companions to a new generation of seekers.

Already published:
Dietrich Bonhoeffer (edited by Robert Coles)
Simone Weil (edited by Eric O. Springsted)
Henri Nouwen (edited by Robert A. Jonas)
Pierre Teilhard de Chardin (edited by Ursula King)
Charles de Foucauld (edited by Robert Ellsberg)

Forthcoming volumes include:
Karl Rahner
Oscar Romero
John Main
Flannery O'Connor
Brother Roger of Taizé

MODERN SPIRITUAL MASTERS SERIES

ANTHONY DE MELLO

*Writings Selected
with an Introduction by*

WILLIAM DYCH, S. J.

Maryknoll, New York 10545

Third Printing, October 2000

The Catholic Foreign Mission Society of America (Maryknoll) recruits and trains people for overseas missionary service. Through Orbis Books, Maryknoll aims to foster the international dialogue that is essential to mission. The books published, however, reflect the opinions of their authors and are not meant to represent the official position of the society.

To obtain more information about Maryknoll and Orbis Books, please visit our website at www.maryknoll.org.

Library of Congress Cataloging-in-Publication Data
De Mello, Anthony, 1931-
   [Selections. 1999]
   Anthony De Mello : writings / selected with an introduction by
William Dych.
     p.   cm. – (Modern spiritual masters series)
   ISBN 1-57075-283-4 (pbk.)
   1. Spiritual life – Catholic Church. 2. Spiritual exercises.
I. Dych, William V.   II. Title.   III. Series.
BX2182.2.D385   1999
248.4′82 – dc21   99-17007

Contents

Introduction

In his later years the Indian Jesuit Father Anthony de Mello spent a good part of every summer in the United States conducting retreats and workshops for ever larger and more responsive audiences. In addition to his appreciation of the lively give-and-take he enjoyed with his audiences, it was the source of no small joy and pride that his preaching was bearing such abundant fruit in a country that for so many years had been sending its own missionaries to India. He was happy that the path of missionary activity between his native India and the United States had become a two-way path, and this not just in a geographical sense. Culturally, spiritually, and theologically, he was convinced, the country from the East and the country from the West had much to give and much to gain from fruitful exchange with each other.

Anthony de Mello was born on September 4, 1931, in Bombay, India, and though he thus shared the birthplace of the British author Rudyard Kipling, he did not share the latter's sentiment that "East is East, and West is West, and never the twain shall meet." In his life and education Anthony de Mello embodied that meeting. He was brought up a Roman Catholic and entered the Jesuit order at the young age of sixteen. After finishing his basic formation as a Jesuit in Bombay, he went abroad for a variety of studies: philosophy in Barcelona, psychology at Loyola University in Chicago, and spiritual theology at the Gregorian University in Rome. With this rich and varied education in the West and his first-hand familiarity with the spiritualities of the East, around 1960 he set out upon what was to become his life-long career of conducting retreats, workshops, conferences, and seminars in spirituality both at home and quite literally around the globe: North America, Europe, Australia, Japan, the Philippines, and beyond.

His base at home was the spiritual center he founded and headed near Poona called "Sadhana," a name that was also to become the title of his first book in 1978. The subtitle, *A Way to God,* throws light on the meaning of the Indian title. Presenting "Christian exercises in Eastern form," the book offers a variety of spiritual exercises, techniques and disciplines designed to help people learn to pray by making the simple discovery that God is already present in their lives. With that discovery and the ensuing sense of God's presence, prayer becomes a response to that presence. Over the next nine years there followed a rich succession of books comprised of stories, spiritual exercises, story meditations, and meditations in the more formal sense. This prolific output was abruptly ended by his sudden and untimely death of a heart attack on June 4, 1987, at Fordham University in New York at the age of fifty-six. Those of us who had lunch with him that day in the Jesuit dining room at Fordham can well attest that at the end he was still full of life, indeed that he died at the height of his powers. The readings that follow will try to give a taste of each of these varied writings and the insights they offer, but first by way of introduction some more general reflections on what might have contributed to Anthony de Mello's extraordinary power and influence and his ability to set people free.

The Power of Story

A master was once unmoved by the complaints of his disciples that, though they listened with pleasure to his parables and stories, they were also frustrated for they longed for something deeper. To all their objections he would simply reply: "You have yet to understand, my friends, that the shortest distance between a human being and truth is a story." So goes one of Anthony de Mello's pieces of "one minute wisdom," as you will read shortly in excerpts from his volume of that name. He very often used stories himself to travel that distance with his listeners, and by everyone's account Anthony de Mello was a consummate storyteller. In his retreats and workshops he could regale his listeners for hours on end with story after story, and to their amazement could do this without the benefit of notes. The skill of his delivery alone, however, would merely make Anthony de Mello a master entertainer, but much more than entertainment was taking place in these gatherings. It was the content of the stories that made the difference, for he was using the stories precisely to open his listeners to the truth.

The content of another piece of one minute wisdom shows the folly of those who "longed for something deeper" than story. A preacher kept saying that "we must put God in our lives." But the master replied: "God is already there. Our business is to recognize this." The profound truth expressed in this story opens the way to a whole new sense of God's presence. This presence ceases to be something sporadic or intermittent to be encountered perhaps only rarely at sacred times and in sacred places, for God is never absent for those who have the eyes to see and the ears to hear. The insight expressed in this story explains something the reader will notice immediately in the readings that follow: Father de Mello's frequent insistence on the need for "awareness," for "being awake," for "being in touch," for getting out of the head and "coming to one's senses." All of these expressions are variations on what the master said above. One does not have to do anything to "get into God's presence," but must "recognize" Who is already there.

Why is God already there? Not because of some abstract philosophical doctrine about an impersonal divine omnipresence, but to put it in Christian terms, because of the "Good News" that God loves all people as God's own people and wants to be with them: "God so loved the world that he sent

his only Son" (John 3:16). But doesn't one have to do something to earn that love? Anthony de Mello's Catholic upbringing
(and that of many others) could suggest that the answer perhaps might be yes: One has to keep the commandments to keep
God's love, or one has to go to confession if one has broken
the commandments. Then the love of God resumes. Tony de
Mello's wry comment, "But then the news is not really all that
good, is it?" rings true to all but the Pharisees among us, who
make themselves pleasing to God through their own efforts. The
insight of the story is that God's love is unconditional and, as
Augustine said, it is God's love that makes us lovable, not our
efforts. It is *awareness* of this, to use a favorite de Mello word
that you will read often below, that can set us free to love in
return. Hence this does not mean that keeping the commandments is not really all that important, but means simply that it
is awareness of God's presence and love that sets us free to love
in return rather than efforts at reform and self-improvement on
our own part.

The Depths of Story

Further reflection on these two stories reveals two further and
deeper dimensions of Anthony de Mello's spiritual thought.
When he says in the first that story is the shortest route to the
truth, he does not mean the abstract truth that is the product
of thinking, but the very concrete truth that is reached only in
an experience of the reality of which the truth speaks and to
which the story points. For example, one can know and assent
to the truth of the doctrine that God loves all men and women
as sons and daughters, but an entirely different kind of knowledge is gained when through awareness one has the experience
of actually being loved by God. It is this latter knowledge, not
the former, to which the psalmist exhorts us when he says,
"Taste and see that the Lord is good" (Ps. 34:8), and of which
John speaks when he says that "the truth will make you free"
(John 8:32). Hence Jesus, too, often taught the people through

story and parable; indeed Matthew says that "he said nothing to them without a parable" (Matt. 13:34). Since Anthony de Mello's goal as spiritual director and retreat giver was to change people, not to change their ideas, that is, to bring them to a realization of the truth rather than to clear and distinct ideas about it, the very concrete images of the story rather that the abstract concepts of doctrine were his favored mode of communication.

Of all the truths to which Anthony de Mello wanted to bring his retreatants to realization, none was more important and more central to his spiritual theology than the truth that comes to expression in the second story and is called in Christian tradition the primacy of grace. "God and God's love are already there," says the story, there to be recognized and accepted. Only an awareness of that presence and that love can set a person free to love in return. In this divine-human relationship the initiative is always God's and the human role is always one of response. This means that we cannot simply make up our minds to do the most important things in life, things like loving or trusting. It must be given us to do them, and this "being given" is what is meant by grace. Hence the goal of a de Mello retreat was not moral reform, but "awareness," for it is the only path that can lead to a real change of persons and not just their behavior. Hence against the master's critics mentioned above who "longed for something deeper" than story, when the goal is realization of truth rather than its explanation, there is no deeper or shorter path to the truth than that provided by the concrete images of story.

The Knowledge of God

Everything we have been saying about the power of story to bring us to concrete realization of the truth, including truth about God, presupposes that God can be known by human beings. This is a proposition that is not altogether self-evident, and in fact one that is problematic in both Eastern and Western religious thought. For God is not simply one being among other beings, even if God is conceived of as the "supreme being," for "supreme" asserts merely a quantitative difference between God and the world. But God is rather *qualitatively* different from any and all finite being. God is the "totally other," and various images have been used to try to express this qualitative difference, however inadequately. God is said to be not a being, but the source and ground of being, or God is the horizon within which all beings exist, or, as this latter image comes to expression in scripture: "In him we live and move and have our being" (Acts 17:28).

If the reality of God is qualitatively different from all other reality, then it follows that God must be known in a way qualitatively different from our knowledge of all other realities. Otherwise, in our knowledge God would be reduced to the level of these other realities and what we would be knowing would not really be God, but a human construct, an idol. If knowing finite realities is a process of grasping or comprehending them, God must be known rather as that which lies beyond all of our capacities to comprehend and grasp. God is known precisely as what we cannot comprehend, as the incomprehensible, as the "known unknown," as mystery. Indeed, it is easy enough to get a sense, as Karl Rahner puts it, that all of our knowing in the sense of what we comprehend is but a little island in a vast sea of the unknown, that if we push all of our most limpid clarities far enough they trail off into obscurity, and that the more we know the more we realize how little we know. Our sense of mystery, and with it our sense of awe and wonder, does not decrease as our knowledge increases, but rather increases. Human beings are never far from mystery, the mystery that in Christian terms we call "God," and "awareness" is the process by which we get in touch with this reality.

Analogy

The point of all this is that Anthony de Mello was acutely conscious that the reality of God lies ever beyond all human ideas, concepts, and language, and that if we forget this our God-talk can degenerate into idol (and idle) talk, however sublime and religious it might be. He was conscious of this from the best of both his Western and Eastern traditions. In the West, for example, God's transcendence vis-à-vis all human concepts comes to expression in what is called the highly analogous nature of all of our knowledge of and language about God. In the thirteenth century, the century that gave us the great Summas of theology, the Fourth Lateran Council (1215) taught, nevertheless, that between creator and creature there can be "no similarity so great that a greater dissimilarity cannot be seen between them." All of our concepts and images are formed and forged in our experience of finite realities, and when we apply them to God by asserting some likeness between God and these realities, the unlikeness between them is even greater. For example, when we say that God is a person, we are affirming that God is in some sense like what we mean when we speak of a human person, but at the same time we must not forget, as Lateran IV put it, that God is more unlike than like a human person. Otherwise, of course, we are speaking of God in naively anthropomorphic language that does not do justice to the transcendence of God, which is so central to both Jewish and Christian tradition: "For my thoughts are not your thoughts, neither are your ways my ways, says the Lord. For as the heavens are higher than the earth, so are my ways higher than your ways and my thoughts than your thoughts" (Isa. 55:8–9).

Anthony de Mello reminds us in *Awareness* that the great theologians of the West acknowledged all of this. Thomas Aquinas, for example, says at the beginning of his *Summa Theologiae:* "About God, we cannot say what He is but rather what He is not. And so we cannot speak about how He is, but rather how He is not." The phrase "cannot say" provided the technical Greek term for this approach to theology which is called "apophatic theology." Apophatic theology proceeds on the insight that we cannot know what God is, but can only know what God is not. It experiences God as the "known unknown" and its emphasis is on the "dissimilarity" between creator and creature of which Lateran IV spoke, whereas "kataphatic" theology stresses the real but lesser similarity between them. Both can be true, but as will often be clear in the readings, Anthony de Mello's own experience led him to stress with the apophatic tradition that the reality of God lies beyond all of our inadequate human concepts and language.

Neti/Neti — Not That/Not That

He also learned to appreciate this approach from the religious traditions of the East, expressed there in its own categories and language as in the simple phrase "not that, not that." Taking the same example of person that we used earlier, if we ask whether God is a person, the answer is "not that" (Lateran IV's "dissimilarity"), but if we were to conclude from this that God is not a person, that would be equally false and we would also have to say "not that" (Lateran IV's similarity). Since our notion of person comes from our experience of finite persons, neither the affirmation that God is a person nor the negation that God is a person can capture the personal reality of God who transcends our human category of person. Hence to do justice to God's transcendence of everything finite we can only say "not that, not that." Another example would be the question of afterlife. Were we to think of this afterlife too univocally as simply a continuation of this life, we would have to deny afterlife: not that. But were we to conclude from this that there is no afterlife, that is equally false, and we would also have to say: not that. When we are dealing with realities that transcend our finite categories like God and what lies beyond death, the affirmation or the negation of a proposition does not entail that its opposite is true, and hence when dealing with such realities we can only say, "not that, not that." Questions about such realities do not admit of simple yes or no answers.

As usual Tony de Mello was able to express this dialectical situation and show people its truth by telling a story. The master always encouraged his disciples to look up at the moon by pointing his finger toward it, but invariably the disciples would look at his finger. "Don't look at my finger," he would exclaim, "look at the moon." The story says so many things in so few words. It says that the reality of God always lies beyond all the "fingers" of our images and concepts that we use to point to God, and says that we are always in danger of getting stuck in the words rather than getting in touch with the reality. It also says, or at least implies, that not all fingers point in the right direction, and that some fingers are more adequate to direct us to God than others. It also says that however inadequate and possibly misleading all of our God-talk is, talk we must and point we must, for it is far better to stutter and stammer about the highest and most important realities we encounter in our experience than to speak with great clarity and precision about the trivialities that we endow with such importance.

God and the Religions

If, indeed, it is true, as Anthony de Mello's earlier story said, that no matter where we are, "God is already there. Our business is to recognize this," and if this is true for everyone at all times and in all places, this raises legitimate questions for anyone whose faith has been nurtured in an entirely different perspective. There is the familiar passage in Paul's letter to the Romans, for example, where he asks how anyone can call upon God ("recognize" in the language of the de Mello story) if they have not believed in God. And how are they to believe in a God of whom they have never heard? And how can they hear if no one preaches, Paul continues, and how can anyone preach if they are not sent? Then he concludes that faith comes from what is heard (*fides ex auditu*), and what is heard comes by the preaching of Christ (Rom. 10:14–15, 17). The process that Paul describes here provides a good description of how many Christians came to understand how they have access to God: God was present and revealed in Jesus, and Jesus is present and revealed in the preaching of the church. The de Mello story seems to call all of this into question: If the story is true, then why Jesus, why the church, why any religion?

In recent decades the Christian churches, including the Catholic Church, have been moving toward a new way of understanding their relationship to the larger and very pluralistic world in which they exist, a pluralism which includes a pluralism of religions. In the Catholic Church this move is most pronounced and most explicit in the teaching of the Second Vatican Council (1962–65). Several of its documents affirm that all people have access to the very same truth which Christians, as Paul says, have heard from Christ. To take but one example from among several passages that clearly make this affirmation, *Gaudium et Spes,* the Pastoral Constitution on the Church in the Modern World, makes a statement which only a few years earlier would have been unthinkable. The Council had been speaking of what members of the church have received from Christ, and then continues: "All this holds true not only for Christians, but for all people of good will in whose hearts grace works in an unseen way. For since Christ died for all people, and since the ultimate vocation of all people is in fact one, and divine, we ought to believe that the Holy Spirit in a manner known only to God offers to every person the possibility of being associated with the paschal mystery [of Jesus]" (no. 22).

The statement leaves many questions about the role of Jesus unanswered, but it does, nevertheless, say something that would have been unthinkable in the church only a few years earlier because it departs in a very radical way from what had been the accepted theology about baptism and the church for many centuries, that is, it departs from what we heard Paul say about the necessity of preaching and hearing about Christ in order to receive the truth. The Christian churches have been forced to abandon their earlier and highly exclusive understanding that God is present in the world only through their ministrations by their encounter with other cultures and other religions that has been made possible in a world suddenly become "a global village" through modern means of communication and travel. They have been forced to acknowledge the same truth that Peter was forced to acknowledge somewhat reluctantly in his encounter with the Roman pagan Cornelius in the early decades of the church's existence. The story is told in the Acts of the Apostles how Peter discovered "that God shows no partiality" among peoples and "does not play favorites" when he witnessed the manifest presence of the Holy Spirit in Cornelius and his household prior to any ministrations on his part (Acts 10:34, 44–45).

This universalism is clearly the spirit of Anthony de Mello's spiritual thought and places him at the forefront of the church's still developing self-understanding. You will be reading later in *The Heart of the Enlightened,* for example, his comment on a story of Plutarch about King Philip and his son, Alexander the Great, who came upon Diogenes the philosopher looking attentively at a heap of human bones. "What are you looking for?" asked Alexander. "Something that I cannot find," said the philosopher. "And what is that?" To this he replied: "The difference between your father's bones and those of his slaves." To which Anthony de Mello adds: "The following are just as indistinguishable: Catholic bones from Protestant bones. Hindu bones from Muslim bones. Arab bones from Israeli bones. Russian bones from American bones." And most importantly, he adds, "Those who are enlightened fail to see the difference even when the bones are clothed in flesh."

Experience and Scripture

How, then, are we to understand the relation between the universal experience of God accessible to all people and what Paul called *fides ex auditu,* that knowledge of God based upon and learned from a particular tradition and its scripture such as the Jewish or Christian Bible or the Muslim Qur'an? First, we must keep in mind that there is no such thing as "pure experience," that is, an experience that has not been shaped by the particular tradition in which a person has been brought up and molded and whose language gives expression to and interprets this person's experience. We are social as well as individual beings. As such, we and our experience are shaped by the society and culture in which we have been reared; without this common culture and language we could not put our experience into words, share it, and belong to a people. This process of communication is essential to our social life together as a people, including as a religious people, so that when the first Christians experienced and interpreted salvation and liberation through the love of Jesus they proclaimed this in the native language of their Jewish scriptures, and eventually formed their own canon of Christian scripture to embody their peculiarly Christian experience. Scripture, then, does not stand over against experience as a body of religious knowledge totally independent of our experience and dictated by God from above, as it were. Rather scripture is the written record of a people's experience, for Christians their experience of Jesus, and it tries to express the knowledge of the God they have encountered in their experience.

Our identity today as Christians, then, is dependent on two equally important factors. First, Christians today must have the same experience of salvation and liberation in Jesus that their forefathers and foremothers had in order to be one people with them, just as the Jewish people today must experience the same liberating power of Yahweh that their forefathers and foremothers experienced in their deliverance from the slavery of Egypt. Second, Christians today need their scriptures as the record of their past in order to keep this past alive and to name their own experience today in light of the formative and paradigmatic experience of their origins. Quoting scripture without sharing the experience of which scripture speaks would simply be formalism and empty words, but isolated, individual experience without word and language to enter into communication with one's people would not be fully human experience. Experience and scripture, then, are not alternate or competing sources of knowledge about God, but are complementary moments in the single process of experiencing the presence of God in one's life and then expressing and interpreting that experience in the language of one's tradition.

Fundamentalism

The complementary relationship of individual and social experience, on the one hand, and the great scriptures of the world in which they come to expression, on the other, can go awry in a variety of ways that Anthony de Mello warns against. One such way that is both perennial in every age and at the same time very pronounced today goes by the name "fundamentalism." Fundamentalism sees its holy book as having been addressed by God exclusively to its adherents directly and immediately, that is, without the mediation of human words or human images and concepts. God's truth has been dictated to a human author who has enshrined it in scripture in test-tube purity. God's word, then, bears no relation to a particular culture and does not bear the mark of a particular time or place or origin, but is an absolute. Such an absolute sees all other people as standing outside the truth and their positions as false and erroneous, and therein lie the roots of the fanatic and the zealot and the seeds of violence.

Anthony de Mello often uses humor to expose and warn against the dangers of this kind of self-centered and solipsistic religious fundamentalism. For example, in *The Song of the Bird* he tells the story of a tourist visiting a town and complimenting his guide on the number of churches he saw. The people here, he says, must surely love the Lord. Perhaps they do love the Lord, replies the guide, "but they sure as hell hate each other." There is also the story, obviously meant to be humorous, about the "World Fair of Religions." At the fair one can visit the Jewish stall and receive a handout saying that God is all-compassionate and that the Jews were his Chosen People. Further along one learns at the Muslim stall that God is all-merciful and Mohammed is his only prophet and that salvation comes from listening to God's only prophet. Moving on to the Christian stall one discovers that God is love and that there is no salvation outside the church. One must join the church or risk eternal damnation. Leaving the fair one visitor asks another what he thinks of God in the light of what the religions say. God is "bigoted, fanatical, and cruel," replies the friend. Back home he said to God: "Why do you put up with this sort of thing? Do you not see that they have been giving you a bad name for centuries?" "I did not organize the fair," replies God, "and I would be too ashamed even to visit it." Humor is probably the most effective weapon against such self-centered fundamentalism, but the more zealous and dogmatic the fundamentalists, the less they are able to see the humor.

In any case, however, the stories do bring out the value and importance of the kind of ecumenical work to which Anthony de Mello dedicated his life by trying to build a bridge of understanding, tolerance, and acceptance between the religions of East and West. He did this, as we have seen, not by theoretical discussion of competing positions or truth-claims, but by using the very practical path of the story to take the shortest route to the truth. It would be a mistake, then, to think that because East and West are different, either the one or the other must be wrong, and that Anthony de Mello wanted to use one in order to "correct" the other. Rather Eastern and Western approaches to the truth are so radically different that they do not fit into the same logical framework so that one could be corrected by the other. Each has a validity of its own and can be used not to correct the other, but to complement the other and give a broader and more balanced approach to the truth. Against the narrow forces of bigotry and intolerance Anthony de Mello was an apostle of balance, of both/and rather than either/or.

Expanding Horizons

It is a hopeful sign of the expanding horizons of Roman Catholic thought and of its more recent attempts to become more truly catholic that what has been viewed as Anthony de Mello's "oriental wisdom" and "Eastern perspective" can be accepted as not only not contradictory to Catholic theology, but as echoing its own sometimes forgotten riches. What is meant by "expanding horizons" can perhaps best be seen in a simple example of its opposite, namely, in the bias at work in a not uncommon reading of the opening verses of the Letter to the Hebrews. The text reads: "In many and various ways God spoke of old to our fathers by the prophets; but in these last days he has spoken to us by a Son ... " (Heb. 1:1–2). The bias I have in mind lies in the tendency to hear this text saying that elsewhere God has been silent, and that it is only in the Jewish prophets and in Jesus that God has addressed humankind. The text, of course, does not say that. It says nothing of God's dealings with humankind outside the Jewish and Christian tradition. This is the bias that Anthony de Mello tries to expose and bring home to biased people in the story we read about the "World Fair of Religions."

If, however, the Hebrews text is heard with Father de Mello and with Peter as he is portrayed in Acts (10:34–36) upon his discovery in the person of the Roman Cornelius that "God does not play favorites" and shows "no partiality" among the nations, not only God's word but also God's grace breaks out of the narrow channels within which some religious people would confine it. For example, however important in the Catholic Church the "seven sacraments" in the strict, technical sense of the term "sacrament" might be, they are not the only and exclusive channels of God's grace. This is the point de Mello is making when he insists that however much we need "holy times" and "holy places," that is, our feasts and festivals, our shrines and our sanctuaries, we must not allow the holy to be limited exclusively to just these times and just these places. We must never forget our Catholic tradition's insistence that "the Spirit blows where the Spirit will," not where we decide or determine. This attitude sees our seven sacraments within a much broader and more comprehensive principle of sacramentality.

This principle maintains that the entire material order of creation can embody, that is, can be the symbol and sacrament of, the presence of the invisible God. It can be this, of course, not in an undifferentiated way. God is universally present, but not everywhere in the same way and to the same intensity. The real presence of Jesus in the Eucharist is for Catholics a particularly intense moment of encounter with the divine presence. But this specifically religious encounter cannot be allowed to obscure the broader and more comprehensive sense in which one must "find God in all things" and encounter Jesus in all of his brothers and sisters (Matt. 25:31–46). The tendency of many to remain confined instead within a narrow, religious sense of divine presence explains the repeated de Mello call: "Awareness, Awareness, Awareness!" Be alive, be awake, be sensitive to the realities right there before your eyes. One can imagine what a difference it would make if all those who profess faith in Jesus and in his passion could become aware of the history of his passion still being played out in the suffering of his brothers and sisters today.

The Presence of the Spirit

The de Mello emphasis on the largesse of divine love which includes all people within the family of God's chosen and God's elect echoes contemporary efforts in Catholic theology to recover the often forgotten role of the Holy Spirit. This forgetfulness results in what has been called an overly exclusive "christocentrism," which places too exclusive a focus on Jesus to the neglect of the work of the Holy Spirit. The historical moment of Jesus, of course, is all important for Christian faith. Like Judaism, Christianity is a historical religion. Its God is not a remote deity dwelling at a distance, but is encountered in history, at particular times and places and in specific persons and situations. For Christians Jesus of Nazareth in his historical existence two thousand years ago was and is the climactic moment of this historical encounter of God and humankind. But however important this person and this moment are, they cannot render all other moments otiose and of no religious account. For God's Spirit has been present and at work throughout all of history creating moments of revelation and grace. Jesus and the Spirit, then, are not competitors, but the particular history of Jesus took place within the larger history of the activity of God's Spirit in the world.

Hence Anthony de Mello can speak of other masters besides Jesus, masters who in other times and other cultures are, nevertheless, part of the same history of God's Spirit in the world as was Jesus himself. In this one history the one Spirit of God speaks always one and the same message of God's love but, as in the case of Jesus, speaks the language of that particular place and culture. Religion, like all things human, is determined and conditioned by the culture where it emerges. It always comes to us as refracted through the minds and imaginations of the people who gave it voice. To deny this is to take the path of fundamentalism, which absolutizes the relative and the finite human word. How these different masters and the different religious languages they speak will one day be seen in the unity of the Spirit is an aspect of the larger cultural question how humankind with all its divisions and differences will one day become the single human family of God's intention and design.

In the meantime we live with these differences, but de Mello refused to accord them any ultimate significance. This is the point he makes in his story about Diogenes, who is unable to find any difference between the bones of the king and those of his slaves. For on the deeper level of our shared human experience of birth and death, of tragedy and triumph, we are all indeed of a piece, the same human piece. The Second Vatican Council points to the distinction of these levels when it treats the notion of tradition in its Constitution on Divine Revelation. Rather than thinking of tradition only as the passing on of teaching, important though this might be, it introduces a deeper level of tradition. The church, the Council says, "must pass on all that she is, and all that she teaches" (*Dei Verbum,* no. 8). In

what she is, that is, in her being and life, the church must be
in touch with the realities about which she teaches. She passes
this on not in words but by being it, and without this deeper
level of tradition the words by themselves can become simply
religious rhetoric.

Accepting the Council's distinction between what the church
is and what she teaches opens the possibility that in the midst of
the differences in teaching that divide us there can be real union
on the level of being and life. This possibility is not a reason for
complacence, but a challenge to work toward the day when we
can speak the same truth as well as live the same truth. In any
case it is this distinction between the church's being and life and
its teaching that enables the Second Vatican Council to make
the universal affirmations we have already mentioned. It affirms
(*Lumen Gentium,* no. 16; *Gaudium et Spes,* no. 22; *Ad Gentes,*
no. 7) that all people, regardless of their religious teaching or
lack of it, can be associated with the paschal mystery of Jesus'
death and resurrection, which is the very heart of the church's
own being and life. This is the deeper level of tradition, the level
of experience where the mystery of Jesus' dying and rising can
be lived in myriad ways and in countless different situations.
In Christian language this is the universal presence of the Spirit
and his offer of grace resounding in the hearts of all people.

Awareness and the Spirit

But the universal presence of the Spirit is to no avail unless, in
de Mello language, people have become "aware." The de Mello
stories are designed, like the parables of Jesus, to jolt people
into seeing things they did not see before, that is, to make them
aware. But why is seeing so difficult? Why is awareness so difficult to achieve? Because it is so difficult to allow the Spirit to
blow where the Spirit will. We are creatures of habit and rou-
tine. We think we know in advance where to expect the Spirit,
and that is the only place we look. Indeed, should the Spirit
blow elsewhere, that is, should the Spirit blow where the Spirit

will and not where we will, our blinders, religious and otherwise, block that out. It is so difficult to be aware of what is
right there in front of our eyes because we prefer to see our
labels for things rather than things themselves — labels that en-
shrine our preconceptions, our prejudices, and our preferences.
To remove these labels, to remove our blinders and to allow the
Spirit to blow where the Spirit will is, indeed, very difficult and
requires a genuine religious conversion, the conversion Anthony
de Mello calls becoming aware.

All those who have embarked upon the journey toward
awareness become ever more attuned to the present where the
Spirit is present and at work. In this sense they know that God
has to be found in the world in which they are living and not
in a distant heaven. They see the challenge of their faith and
hope not so much as a theoretical challenge as it is a practical challenge to do the truth here and now. Here, too, de
Mello's spiritual thought echoes the teaching of the Second Vatican Council, which reminds Christians that their eschatological
hope in God's future kingdom must not diminish, but must en-
hance the importance of inner-worldly realities and hopes here
and now.

Conclusion

We can summarize what we have singled out as some of the
main features of Anthony de Mello's spiritual thought within
the framework of the Christian doctrine of the Trinity. First,
he places great emphasis on the "beyondness" of God, God's
transcendence of this world and everything in it. As the totally other, God is incomprehensible, beyond our capacity to
grasp and comprehend. We know God as the mystery in whom
"we live and move and have our being" (Acts 17:28), that is,
God is the "known unknown." This does not render us totally silent, but it is a constant warning against absolutizing
human concepts, human images, human formulas, or any of
our human constructs and making them idols. Our penchant

for turning so many things, religious and otherwise, into idols
shows how difficult it is to worship only one God. It is this
aspect of God, God's utter transcendence, that comes to expression in the names by which we designate the first person of the
Trinity, namely, God as Father/Mother, the creator and source
of all things visible and invisible.

But equally important and equally primordial in the Christian understanding of God as interpreted by Anthony de Mello
is the immanence of God, that is, God's presence within and
throughout God's creation. This is the aspect of God that Augustine points to when he says that God is closer to us than
we are to ourselves. Transcendence, then, does not connote distance, but God's sovereign freedom in choosing to be this close
to us. Without this immanence the transcendent God becomes
the distant God of deism, whereas without transcendence the
immanence of God becomes some form of pantheism. It is this
immanence that we designate by the name God as Spirit.

This Spirit is present universally not just in the sense of *all*
people, but also in the sense of *everything* human. The Spirit is
present not in a separate compartment of life called the religious
or the spiritual, to be carefully demarcated from the secular and
the profane, for nothing human is foreign to the Spirit. This we
learn from the Incarnation: The Word of God became flesh in
Jesus and thereby revealed the ultimate destiny of all flesh and
of everything human. This aspect of God we designate by the
name Son. In Jesus and with Jesus, all men and women, of all
religions and no religion, are called to be sons and daughters of
the one God who "does not play favorites" (Acts 10:34). Such
is the very catholic vision of Anthony de Mello, a vision that
inspires and animates the readings that follow.

1

Sadhana — A Way to God

Christian Exercises in Eastern Form

Introduction

I have spent the past fifteen years of my life as a retreat master and spiritual director helping people to pray. I hear dozens of people complain that they do not know how to pray; that, in spite of all their efforts, they seem to make no progress in prayer; that they find prayer dull and frustrating. I hear many spiritual directors confess helplessness when it comes to teaching people how to pray or, to put it more exactly, how to get satisfaction and fulfillment from prayer.

This always amazes me because I have found it relatively easy to help people to pray. I do not attribute this merely to some personal charisma I have. I attribute it to some very simple theories that I follow in my own prayer life and in guiding others in the matter of prayer. One theory is that prayer is an exercise that brings fulfillment and satisfaction and it is perfectly legitimate to seek these from prayer. Another is that prayer is to be made less with the head than with the heart. In fact, the sooner it gets away from the head and from thinking the more enjoyable and the more profitable it is likely to become. Most priests and religious equate prayer with thinking. That is their downfall.

A Jesuit friend once told me that he approached a Hindu guru for initiation in the art of prayer. The guru said to him, "Concentrate on your breathing." My friend proceeded to do just that for about five minutes. Then the guru said, "The air you breathe is God. You are breathing God in and out. Become aware of that, and stay with that awareness." My friend, after mentally making a slight theological adjustment to that statement, followed these instructions — for hours on end, day after day — and discovered, to his amazement, that prayer can be as simple a matter as breathing in and out. And he discovered in this exercise a depth and satisfaction and spiritual nourishment that he hadn't found in the many, many hours he had devoted to prayer over a period of many years.

Body Sensations

One of the biggest enemies to prayer is nervous tension. This exercise helps you to deal with that. The formula is a simple one: You relax when you come to your senses, when you become as fully conscious as possible of your body sensations, of the sounds around you, of your breathing, of the taste of something in your mouth.

Far too many people live too much *in their head* — they are mostly conscious of the thinking and fantasizing that is going on in their head and far too little conscious of the activity of their senses. As a result they rarely live in the present. They are almost always in the past or in the future. In the past, regretting past mistakes, feeling guilty about past sins, gloating over past achievements, resenting past injuries caused them by other people. Or in the future, dreading possible calamities and unpleasantnesses, anticipating future joys, dreaming of future events.

Recalling the past in order to profit from it, or even to enjoy it afresh, and anticipating the future in order to plan realistically are valuable functions, provided they do not take us out of the present for too long. To succeed in prayer it is essential to develop the ability to make contact with the present and to stay there. And there is no better method I know of for staying in the present than getting out of your head and returning to your senses.

Feel the heat or cold of the atmosphere around you. Feel the breeze as it caresses your body. Feel the heat of the sun making contact with your skin. Feel the texture and temperature of the object you are touching...and see what a difference it makes. See how you come alive by coming to the present. Once you have mastered this technique of sense awareness you will be surprised to see what it does to you if you are the type that frequently worries about the future or feels guilty about the past.

A word about getting out of your head: The head is not a very good place for prayer. It is not a bad place for *starting* your prayer. But if your prayer stays there too long and doesn't move into the heart, it will gradually dry up and prove tiresome and frustrating. You must learn to move out of the area of thinking and talking and move into the area of feeling, sensing, loving, intuiting. That is the area where contemplation is born and prayer becomes a transforming power and a source of never-ending delight and peace.

Awareness and Contemplation

This, perhaps, is the time to deal with the objection, sometimes raised in my Contemplation Groups, that these awareness exercises, while they may help for relaxation, have nothing to do with contemplation in the way we Christians understand the word, and most certainly are not prayer.

I shall now attempt to explain how these simple exercises can be taken to be contemplation in the strict Christian sense of the word. If the explanation does not satisfy you or only creates problems for you, then I suggest that you put aside all I say about this matter and practice these awareness exercises merely as a means for disposing yourself for prayer and contemplation, or just ignore these exercises altogether and move on to others in this book that are more to your taste.

Let me first explain my use of the words "prayer" and "contemplation." I use the word prayer to mean communication with God that is carried on mainly through the use of words and images and thoughts. I shall propose many exercises, later on, that I consider to come under the heading of prayer. Contemplation for me is communication with God that makes a minimal use of words, images, and concepts or dispenses with words, images, and concepts altogether. This is the sort of prayer that John of the Cross speaks of in his *Dark Night of the Soul* or the author of *The Cloud of Unknowing* explains in his admirable book. Some of the exercises that I propose in this book connected with the Jesus Prayer could be considered to be either prayer or contemplation or a blending of both, depending on how much emphasis you place on words and thoughts in your use of the exercises.

And now to the heart of our problems: When I practice the exercise of being aware of my body sensations or of my breathing, can I be said to be communicating with God? The answer is yes. Let me explain the nature of this *communicating* with God that takes place in the awareness exercises.

Many mystics tell us that, in addition to the mind and heart with which we ordinarily communicate with God, we are, all of us, endowed with a mystical mind and mystical heart, a faculty which makes it possible for us to know God directly, to grasp and *intuit* him in his very being, though in a dark manner, apart from all thoughts and concepts and images.

Ordinarily all our contact with God is indirect — through images and concepts that necessarily distort his reality. To be able to grasp him beyond these thoughts and images is the privilege of this faculty which, in the course of this explanation, I shall call the Heart (a word dear to the author of *The Cloud of Unknowing*, though it has nothing to do with our physical heart or our affectivity).

In most of us this Heart lies dormant and undeveloped. If it were to be awakened it would be constantly straining toward God and, given a chance, would impel the whole of our being toward him. But for this, it needs to be developed, it needs to have the dross that surrounds it removed so that it can be attracted toward the Eternal Magnet.

The dross is the vast number of thoughts and words and images that we constantly interpose between ourselves and God when we are communicating with him. Words sometimes serve to impede rather than foster communication and intimacy. Silence — of words and thoughts — can sometimes be the most powerful form of communication and union when hearts are full of love. Our communication with God, however, is not quite so simple a matter. I can gaze lovingly into the eyes of an intimate friend and communicate with him beyond words. But what do I gaze into when I gaze silently at God? An imageless, formless reality. A blank!

Now that is just what is demanded of some people if they would go deep into communion with the infinite, with God: Gaze for hours at a blank. Some mystics recommend that we gaze at this blank *lovingly*. And it requires a good deal of faith to gaze with love and yearning at what seems like just nothing when we first get in touch with it.

Ordinarily you will never even get anywhere near this blank, even supposing an intense desire on your part to spend hours on end gazing at it, if your mind isn't silenced. As long as your mind machine keeps spinning out millions of thoughts and words, your *mystical mind,* or Heart, will remain underdeveloped. Notice how sharp is the hearing and the sense of touch of a blind man. He has lost his faculty of seeing and this has forced him to develop his other faculties of perception. Something similar happens in the mystical world. If we could go mentally blind, so to speak, if we could put a bandage over our mind while we are communicating with God, we would be forced to develop some other faculty for communicating with him — that faculty which, according to a number of mystics, is already straining to move out to him anyway if it were given a chance to develop: the Heart.

When our Heart gets its first direct, dark glimpse of God, it feels like a glimpse into emptiness and blankness. People who get to this stage frequently complain that they are doing nothing at prayer, that they are wasting their time, that they are idle, that nothing seems to happen, that they are in total darkness. To escape from this uncomfortable state they, unfortunately, have recourse once again to their thinking faculty; they take the bandage off their minds and begin to *think* and to *speak* with God — just the one thing they need *not* do.

If God is gracious to them, and he very frequently is, he will make it impossible for them to use their mind in prayer. They will find all thinking distasteful; vocal prayer will be unbearable to them because the words seem meaningless; they will just go *dry* every time they attempt to communicate with God in any way except the way of silence. And initially even this silence is painful and dry. They might then slip into the biggest evil of all: They may abandon prayer altogether because they find themselves forced, in prayer, to choose between the frustration of not being able to use their minds and the hollow feeling of wasting their time and doing nothing in the darkness that meets them when they silence their minds.

If they avoid this evil and persevere in the exercise of prayer and expose themselves, in blind faith, to the emptiness, the darkness, the idleness, the nothingness, they will gradually discover, at first in small flashes, later in a more permanent fashion, that there is a glow in the darkness, that the emptiness mysteriously fills their heart, that the idleness is full of God's activity, that in the nothingness their being is recreated and shaped anew . . . and all of this in a way they just cannot describe either to themselves or to others. They will just know after each such session of prayer or contemplation, call it what you will, that something mysterious has been working within them, bringing refreshment and nourishment and well-being with it. They will notice they have a yearning hunger to return to this dark contemplation that seems to make no sense and yet fills them with life, even with a mild intoxication that they can hardly perceive with their mind, they can hardly feel with their emotions, and yet is unmistakably there and so real and satisfying that they wouldn't exchange it for all the intoxication that comes from the delights that the world of the senses and the emotions and the mind has to offer. Funny that at the beginning it should have seemed so dry and dark and tasteless!

If you would attain to this state and draw close to this mystical darkness and begin to communicate with God through this Heart that the mystics speak of, the first thing you may have to do is find some means for silencing the mind. There are some fortunate people (and it is very important that you know this lest you fall into the error of thinking that everyone who would make progress in contemplation must, of necessity, pass through this process of confronting the darkness) who attain to this spontaneously without ever having to silence their discursive mind and quiet all their words and thoughts. They are like people who have all the sharpness of the blind man in their hands and ears and yet continue to enjoy the full use of their sight. They relish vocal prayer, they profit immensely from the use of their imagination in prayer, they give full rein to their thought processes while they deal with God, and beneath all this activity their Heart develops and directly intuits the divine.

If you are not among these fortunate people, you will have to do something to develop this Heart of yours. There is nothing you can do directly. All you can do is silence your discursive mind: Abstain from all thoughts and words while you are at prayer and leave the Heart to develop by itself.

To silence the mind is an extremely difficult task. How hard it is to keep the mind from thinking, thinking, thinking, forever thinking, forever producing thoughts in a never-ending stream. Our Hindu masters in India have a saying: One thorn is removed by another. By this they mean that you will be wise to use one thought to rid yourself of all the other thoughts that crowd into your mind. One thought, one image, one phrase or sentence or word that your mind can be made to fasten on. For to consciously attempt to keep the mind in a *thought-less* state, in a void, is to attempt the impossible. The mind must have something to occupy it. Well, then, give it something with which to occupy itself — but just one thing. An image of the Savior that you gaze on lovingly and to which you return each time you are distracted; an ejaculation that you keep repeating ceaselessly to prevent the mind from wandering. A time will come, hopefully, when the image will disappear from consciousness, when the word will be taken out of your mouth and your discursive mind will be perfectly stilled and your Heart will be given free scope to gaze, unimpeded, into the Darkness!

As a matter of fact, you do not even have to get to this stage where the image disappears and the words are stilled to have your Heart function. The fact that your discursive mind has had its activity reduced so drastically is already an immense help for the Heart to develop and to function. So even if you never get to the imageless and the wordless state you will, quite likely, be growing in contemplation.

You will notice that the two means I have suggested, the image of the Savior and the repetition of an ejaculation, are both overtly *religious* in nature. Keep in mind, however, that our primary purpose in this exercise is not the type of activity that the discursive mind engages in, but the opening up and developing of the Heart. Provided this is achieved, does it really matter whether the *thorn* you use to remove all the other thorns is a religious thorn or not? If your main purpose is to get light into your darkness, does it really matter that the candle that sheds light into your darkness is a holy candle or not? Does it matter, then, whether you concentrate on an image of the Savior or a book or a leaf or a spot on the floor? A Jesuit friend who loves to dabble in such things (and, I suspect, test all religious theories with a healthy measure of skepticism) assures me that, through constantly saying to himself "one-two-three-four" rhythmically, he achieves the same *mystical* results that his more *religious* confreres claim to achieve through the devout and rhythmical recitation of some ejaculations! And I believe him. There is, undoubtedly, a sacramental value in the use of the *religious* thorn. But as far as our main purpose is concerned, one thorn is just as good as another.

And so we are led to the seemingly disconcerting conclusion that concentration on your breathing or your body sensations is very good contemplation in the strict sense of the word. I have had this theory of mine confirmed by some Jesuits who made a thirty-day retreat under my guidance and who agreed to give, in addition to the five hours that they were supposed to give to what we call the Ignatian exercises, four or five hours a day to this simple exercise of awareness of their breathing and of their body sensations. I was not surprised when they told me that during their awareness exercises (once they had developed some familiarity with them) their experiences were identical with the experiences they had while practicing what is known in Catholic terminology as the prayer of faith, or the prayer of quiet. Most of them even assured me that these awareness exercises led to a deepening of the prayer experiences they had formerly had, giving these experiences more vigor and sharpness, in a manner of speaking....

I would not have you abandon all your prayer (communication with God that involves the use of words, images, and concepts) in favor of *pure contemplation*. There is a time for meditation and prayer and there is a time for contemplation, just as there is a time for action and a time for contemplation. While you are engaged in what I have called *contemplation,* however, make sure you do not give in to the temptation to think — no matter how holy the thought may be. Just as in your time of prayer you would reject *holy* thoughts that are connected with your work and which are very good at their own proper time but are now a distraction to your prayer, so in your time of contemplation you must vigorously reject all thoughts of whatever nature as being destructive of this particular form

of communication with God. Now is the time to expose yourself to the divine sun in silence, not to reflect on the virtues and
properties of the sun's rays; now is the time to gaze lovingly into
the eyes of your divine lover and not break this special intimacy
with words and reflections about him. Communication through
words must be put off for another occasion. Now is the time
for wordless communion.

There is one important point on which I cannot, unfortunately, give you guidance. For this you will need the guidance of
an experienced master who is familiar with your spiritual needs.
The point is: How much of the time that you set aside daily
for communion with God should you give to prayer and how
much to contemplation. This is something you can best decide
with your spiritual director. With his help you will also have to
decide whether you should go in for this kind of *contemplation*
at all. Perhaps you are one of those fortunate people I spoke of
earlier who have the fullest use of their hands and ears without ever having to bandage their eyes; whose mystical Heart is
in the deepest possible communion with God while their mind
communicates with him through words and thoughts; who do
not need to keep silence to achieve, with their Beloved, the kind
of intimacy that many others achieve only through silence. . . .

Breath Communication with God

Earlier I made a distinction between prayer and contemplation. There is another way of expressing that distinction —
by speaking of two types of prayer, the devotional and the
intuitional.

Intuitional prayer would coincide roughly with what I called
contemplation, devotional prayer with what I called prayer.
Both forms of prayer lead to union with God. Each of them is
more suited to some people than to others. Or the same people
will find one form of prayer more suitable to their needs at one
time rather than at another.

Devotional prayer too is geared to the heart, for any prayer that limits itself to the thinking mind alone is not prayer really but, at best, a preparation for prayer. Even among men there is no genuine personal communication that isn't at least in some small degree heart communication, that does not contain some small degree of emotion in it. If a communication, a sharing of *thoughts,* is entirely and totally devoid of all emotion, you can be sure the intimate, personal dimension is lacking. There is no communion leading to intimacy.

I want to give you now a variation of the previous exercise that will make the exercise more devotional than intuitional. You will notice, however, that the amount of thought content in the prayer is minimal, and so the exercise will easily move from the devotional to the intuitional, from the heart to the Heart. It will become, in fact, a good combination of the devotional and the intuitional.

Become aware of your breathing for a while . . .

Now reflect on the presence of God in the atmosphere all around you. . . . Reflect on his presence in the air you are breathing. . . . Be conscious of his presence in the air as you breathe in and out. . . . Notice what you feel when you become conscious of his presence in the air you are breathing in and out.

I want you now to express yourself to God. But I want you to do this nonverbally. Frequently, expressing a sentiment through a look or a gesture makes the expression much more powerful than expressing it through words. I want you to express various sentiments to God not through words but through your breathing.

Express, first of all, a great yearning for him. Without using any words, even mentally, say to him, "My God, I long for you . . . " just by the way you breathe. Perhaps you will express this by breathing in deeply, by deepening your inhalation. . . .

Now express another attitude or sentiment: one of trust and surrender. Without any words, just through the way you breathe, say to him, "My God, I surrender myself entirely to you. . . . " You may want to do this by emphasizing your exhalation, by breathing out each time as if you were sighing deeply.

Each time you breathe out, feel yourself letting the whole of yourself go in God's hands....

Now take up other attitudes before God and express these through your breathing. Love...Closeness and Intimacy... Adoration...Gratitude...Praise....

If you tire of doing this, return to the beginning of this exercise and just rest peacefully in the awareness of God all around you and in the air you are breathing in and out....There, if you tend to get distracted, fall back on the second part of the exercise and express yourself to God nonverbally once more....

The ability to see God's activity in everything was something typical of the Hebrew mentality we find in the Bible. Where we seem to dwell almost exclusively on secondary causes, the Hebrews seemed to dwell almost exclusively on the Primary Cause. Were their armies defeated in battle? It was God who defeated them, not the ineptness of their generals! Did it rain? It was God who made the rain fall. Were their crops destroyed by locusts? It was God who sent the locusts. Even more daringly they would speak of God hardening the hearts of wicked men!

Their view of reality was, admittedly, partial. They seemed to ignore secondary causes entirely. Our modern view of reality is equally, and more grossly, partial, for we seem to ignore the Primary Cause entirely. Has your headache disappeared? Where the Hebrew would have said, "God cured you," we say, "Leave God out of this; the aspirin tablet cured you." The reality is that it was God who cured you through the aspirin tablet, of course. We have, however, all but lost our sense of the Infinite operating within our lives. We no longer sense God guiding us to our destiny through our rulers, God healing us of our emotional wounds through our counselors, God bringing us health through our physicians, God shaping every event that we meet, God sending every person who enters our life, God producing the rain, God playing about us in the breeze and touching us in every sensation we feel and producing sounds all around us so that they shall be registered on our eardrums and we shall hear him!

Personal Benefits from Awareness

When you first start out on the type of contemplation proposed in the exercises that have preceded, you are likely to have misgivings regarding the value of these exercises. They seem to be neither meditation nor prayer in the traditional sense of the words. If prayer is understood as *speaking with God,* there is very little or no speaking at all here. If meditation is taken to mean reflection, lights and insights, resolutions, then there is hardly any scope for meditation in these exercises.

You come away from these exercises with nothing concrete to show for all the effort you put into them. Nothing you can write about in your spiritual diary — at least not at the beginning and, maybe, not ever. You will frequently come away with the uneasy feeling that you have done nothing and achieved nothing. This form of prayer is particularly painful to the young and to those who set great store by achievement — people to whom effort is more important than just being.

I vividly remember one young person who seemed to attain nothing from these exercises. He found it very frustrating to have to sit down motionless and expose himself to a blank, even though he admitted that he simply could not think or use his mind in any other way while he was at prayer. He would spend most of the time that he dedicated to these exercises in dealing with distractions — generally unsuccessfully — and he pleaded with me to offer him something that would make the time and effort he expended in prayer seem more worth his while. He fortunately persevered in these seemingly frustrating exercises, and after some six months he came to report to me that he was drawing immense benefit from them — far more than he had ever attained from his former prayers and meditations and lights and resolutions. What had happened? He was certainly finding a greater peace in these exercises. His distractions had not diminished. He was finding the exercises as frustrating as before. Nothing had changed in the exercises. What had changed was his life! This constant, painful, distraction-ridden attempt he was making day after day to expose himself to what seemed to be nothingness and emptiness, to attempt to just quiet his mind and attain some sort of silence through concentration on body sensations or breathing or sounds, was bringing him a new power in his daily living that he hadn't noticed there before — and power in so great a measure that its presence in his life was unmistakable.

This is one of the major benefits of this form of prayer: a change in oneself that seems effortless. All the virtues you formerly tried to attain through the exercise of your *will power* seem to come to you effortlessly now — sincerity, simplicity, kindliness, patience.... Addictions seem to drop off without the need for resolutions and effort on one's part: thing addictions like smoking and the excessive use of alcohol, person addictions like infatuations and overdependency.

When this happens to you, you will know that the time investment you made in these exercises is yielding rich dividends....

The Joyful Mysteries of Your Life

Each of us carries in our heart an album of lovely pictures of the past: memories of events that brought gladness to us. I want you now to open this album and recall as many of these events as you can....

If you have never done this exercise before, you are not likely to find many such events at the first try. But you will gradually discover more and more buried away in your past and you will enjoy unearthing them and reliving them in the presence of the Lord. What is more, when new events come to bring you happiness you will cherish the memory of them and not allow them to get lost easily and you will carry around with you an immense treasury into which you can dip any time you wish to bring new joy and vigor to your living.

I imagine this is what Mary did when she carefully placed

away within her heart precious memories of the infancy of
Christ, memories to which she would lovingly return.

Return to some scene in which you felt deeply loved.... How
was this love shown to you? In words, looks, gestures, an act
of service, a letter...? Stay with the scene as long as you experience something of the joy that was yours when the event
took place.

Return to some scene in which you felt joy.... What produced this joy in you? Good news?.... The fulfillment of some
desire?... A scene of nature?.... Recapture the original scene
and the feelings that accompanied it.... Stay as long as you can
with these feelings....

This return to past scenes where you felt love and joy is one
of the finest exercises I know for building up your psychological
health. Many of us go through what one psychologist calls *peak
experiences.* The pity is that when the experience actually takes
place very few people have the capacity to surrender themselves
to it. So they take in nothing of the experience, or very little.
What they need to do is return to these experiences in fantasy
and gradually take the experience in to the full. If you do this you
will discover that, no matter how often you return to these experiences, you will always find in them a supply of nourishment.
Their store never seems to get exhausted. They are a joy forever.

Make sure, however, that you do not return to these scenes
and observe them from the outside, so to speak. They have to be
relived, not observed. Act them out again, participate in them
again. Let the fantasy be so vivid that it is as if the experience is
actually taking place right now for the first time.

It won't be long before you experience the psychological value
of this exercise and you acquire a new respect for fantasy as
a source of life and energy. Fantasy is a very powerful tool for
therapy and personality growth. If it is grounded on reality (when
you fantasize events and scenes that have actually taken place), it
has the same effect (pleasurable or painful) that reality itself has.
If in the dim light of evening I see a friend coming toward me,
and I imagine him to be an enemy, all my reactions, psychological

and physiological, will be the same as if the enemy were really there. If a thirsty man in the desert imagines he sees water, the effect on him will be exactly the same as the effect caused by his seeing real water. When you return to scenes where you felt love and joy, you will enjoy all the benefits that come from being exposed to love and joy . . . and the benefits are immense.

What is the spiritual significance of an exercise like this? In the first place, it breaks down the instinctive resistance that most people have to taking in love and joy. It increases their capacity for accepting love and welcoming joy into their lives. And so it increases their capacity for experiencing God and for opening their hearts to his love and to the happiness that the experience of him brings with it. He who will not allow himself to feel loved by the brother whom he sees, how will he allow himself to feel loved by the God he does not see?

In the second place, this exercise helps overcome the inherent sense of worthlessness, of unworthiness, of guilt, which is one of the principal obstacles that we place in the way of God's grace. In fact, the primary effect of God's grace when it enters our hearts is to make us feel intensely loved — and lovable. Exercises like this one prepare the soil for this grace by making us ready to accept the fact that we are lovable.

Here is another way to draw spiritual benefit from this exercise:

Relive one of these scenes where you felt deeply loved or where you felt deep joy. . . .
Seek and find the presence of the Lord in this scene. . . .
In what form is he present?
This is one way of learning how to find God in all the events of your life, past and present.

A Final Story

There is a Chinese story of an old farmer who had an old horse for tilling his fields. One day the horse escaped into the hills and when all the farmer's neighbors sympathized with the old man over his bad luck, the farmer replied, "Bad luck? Good luck? Who knows?" A week later the horse returned with a herd of wild horses from the hills and this time the neighbors congratulated the farmer on his good luck. His reply was, "Good luck? Bad luck? Who knows?" Then, when the farmer's son was attempting to tame one of the wild horses, he fell off its back and broke his leg. Everyone thought this very bad luck. Not the farmer, whose only reaction was, "Bad luck? Good luck? Who knows?" Some weeks later the army marched into the village and conscripted every able-bodied youth they found there. When they saw the farmer's son with his broken leg they let him off. Now was that good luck? Bad luck? Who knows?

Everything that seems on the surface to be an evil may be a good in disguise. And everything that seems good on the surface may really be an evil. So we are wise when we leave it to God to decide what is good luck and what bad, and thank him that all things turn out for good with those who love him. Then we will share something of that marvelous mystical vision of Dame Julian of Norwich, who uttered the loveliest and most consoling sentence I have ever read: "Sin is behovely, but all shall be well and all shall be well and all manner of thing shall be well."

2

The Song of the Bird

Everyone loves stories, and you will find plenty of them in this book. Stories that are Buddhist, Christian, Zen, Hasidic, Russian, Chinese, Hindu, Sufi; stories ancient and contemporary. And they all have a special quality: If read in a certain kind of way, they will produce spiritual growth.

How to Read to Them

There are three ways:

1. Read a story once. Then move on to another story. This manner of reading will give you only entertainment.

2. Read a story twice. Reflect on it. Apply it to your life. This will give you a taste of theology. This sort of thing can be fruitfully done in a group where all members share their reflections on the story. You then have a theological circle.

3. Read the story again, after you have reflected on it. Create a silence within you and let the story reveal to you its inner depth and meaning: something beyond words and reflections. This will give you a feel for the mystical. Or carry the story around all day and allow its *fragrance,* its *melody* to haunt you. Let it speak to your heart, not to your brain. This too could make something of a mystic

out of you. It is with this mystical end in view that most of these stories were originally told.

Caution

Most of the stories have a comment appended to them. The comment is meant as a sample of the kind of comment you yourself may want to make. Make your own. Don't limit yourself to the ones you find in this book. Why borrow someone else's insights?

Beware of applying the story to anyone (priest, mullah, church, neighbor) other than yourself. If you do so the story will do you damage. Every one of these stories is about *you*, no one else.

Glossary

Theology: The art of telling stories about the divine. Also the art of listening to them.

Mysticism: The art of tasting and feeling in your heart the inner meaning of such stories to the point that they transform you.

Eat Your Own Fruit

A disciple once complained, "You tell us stories, but you never reveal their meaning to us."

Said the master, "How would you like it if someone offered you fruit and masticated it before giving it to you?"

No one can find your meaning for you. Not even the master.

The Song of the Bird

The disciples were full of questions about God.

Said the master, "God is the Unknown and the Unknowable. Every statement about him, every answer to your questions, is a distortion of the truth."

The disciples were bewildered. "Then why do you speak about him at all?"

"Why does the bird sing?" said the master.

Not because it has a statement, but because it has a song.

The words of the scholar are to be understood. The words of the master are not to be understood. They are to be listened to as one listens to the wind in the trees and the sound of the river and the song of the bird. They will awaken something within the heart that is beyond all knowledge.

True Spirituality

The master was asked, "What is spirituality?"

He said, "Spirituality is that which succeeds in bringing one to inner transformation."

"But if I apply the traditional methods handed down by the masters, is that not spirituality?"

"It is not spirituality if it does not perform its function for you. A blanket is no longer a blanket if it does not keep you warm."

"So spirituality does change?"

"People change and needs change. So what was spirituality once is spirituality no more. What generally goes under the name of spirituality is merely the record of past methods."

Don't cut the person to fit the coat.

Did You Hear That Bird Sing?

Hindu India developed a magnificent image to describe God's relationship with creation. God "dances" creation. He is the dancer, creation is his dance. The dance is different from the dancer; yet it has no existence apart from him. You cannot take it home in a box if it pleases you. The moment the dancer stops, the dance ceases to be.

In our quest for God, we think too much, reflect too much, talk too much. Even when we look at this dance that we call creation, we are the whole time thinking, talking (to ourselves and others), reflecting, analyzing, philosophizing. Words. Noise.

Be silent and contemplate the dance. Just look: a star, a flower, a fading leaf, a bird, a stone...any fragment of the dance will do. Look. Listen. Smell. Touch. Taste. And, hopefully, it won't be long before you see him—the dancer himself!

The disciple was always complaining to his master, "You are hiding the final secret of Zen from me." And he would not accept the master's denials.

One day they were walking in the hills when they heard a bird sing.

"Did you hear that bird sing?" said the master.

"Yes," said the disciple.

"Well, now you know that I have hidden nothing from you."

"Yes."

If you really heard a bird sing, if you really saw a tree...you would know. Beyond words and concepts.

What was that you said? You have heard dozens of birds sing and seen hundreds of trees? Ah, was it the tree you saw or the label? If you look at a tree and see a tree, you have really not seen the tree. When you look at the tree and see a miracle—then, at last, you have seen! Did your heart never fill with wordless wonder when you heard a bird in song?

The Bamboos

Brownie, our dog, sat looking up the tree, ears cocked, tail tensely wagging. He was attending to a monkey. No thought disturbed his total concentration, no worry for tomorrow. Brownie was the nearest thing to pure contemplation that I have ever seen.

You may have experienced some of this yourself when you were totally absorbed watching a cat at play. Here is a formula

*for contemplation, as good as any I know: Be totally in the
present. Drop every thought of the future, drop every thought
of the past, drop every image and abstraction, and come into
the present. Contemplation will arise!*

After years of training, the disciple begged his master to give
him enlightenment. The master led him to a bamboo grove and
said, "See that bamboo, how tall it is? See that other one there,
how short it is?"
And the disciple was enlightened.

*They say Buddha practiced every form of asceticism known
to the India of his times, in an effort to attain enlightenment.
All in vain. One day he sat under a bodhi tree and enlightenment occurred. He passed on the secret of enlightenment to his
disciples in words that must seem strange to the uninitiated:
"When you draw in a deep breath, O monks, be aware that
you are drawing in a deep breath. And when you draw in a
shallow breath, O monks, be aware that you are drawing in a
shallow breath. And when you draw in a medium-sized breath,
O monks, be aware that you are drawing in a medium-sized
breath." Awareness. Attention. Absorption.*

*This kind of absorption one observes in little children. They
are close to the Kingdom.*

Holiness in the Present Moment

*Buddha was once asked, "What makes a person holy?" He re-
plied, "Every hour is divided into a certain number of seconds
and every second into a certain number of fractions. Anyone
who is able to be totally present in each fraction of a second is
holy."*

The Japanese warrior was captured by his enemies and
thrown into prison. At night he could not sleep for he was
convinced that he would be tortured the next morning.

Then the words of the master came to his mind. "Tomorrow is not real. The only reality is now."

So he came to the present — and fell asleep.

The person over whom the future has lost its grip. How like the birds of the air and the lilies of the field. No anxieties for tomorrow. Total presence in the now. Holiness!

The Word Made Flesh

In the Gospel of St. John we read:

> The Word became flesh; he came to dwell among us...
> through him all things came to be; no single thing was cre-
> ated without him. All that came to be was alive with his
> life, and that life was the light of men. The light shines on
> in the dark, and the darkness has never quenched it.

Look steadily at the *darkness*. It won't be long before you see the light. Gaze at things. It won't be long before you see the Word.

The Word became flesh; he came to dwell among us....

And stop those frantic efforts to change flesh back into words. Words, words, words!

Searching in the Wrong Place

A neighbor found Nasruddin on hands and knees.

"What are you searching for, Mullah?"

"My key."

Both men got on their knees to search. After a while the neighbor said, "Where did you lose it?"

"At home."

"Good Lord! Then why are you searching here?"

"Because it's brighter here."

Search for God where you lost him.

Label Makers

Life is like heady wine. Everyone reads the label on the bottle. Hardly anyone tastes the wine.

Buddha once held up a flower to his disciples and asked each of them to say something about it.

One pronounced a lecture. Another a poem. Yet another a parable. Each trying to outdo the other in depth and erudition.

Label makers!

Mahakashyap smiled and said nothing. Only he had seen the flower.

If I could only taste a bird, a flower, a tree, a human face! But, alas, I have no time! My energy is spent deciphering the label.

The Formula

The mystic was back from the desert. "Tell us," they said, "what God is like."

But how could he ever tell what he had experienced in his heart? Can God be put into words?

He finally gave them a formula — so inaccurate, so inadequate — in the hope that some of them might be tempted to experience it for themselves.

They seized upon the formula. They made it a sacred text. They imposed it on others as a holy belief. They went to great pains to spread it in foreign lands. Some even gave their lives for it.

The mystic was sad. It might have been better if he had said nothing.

The Medal

A mother could not get her son to come home before sunset. So she told him that the road to their house was haunted by ghosts who came out after dark.

By the time the boy grew up he was so afraid of ghosts that he refused to run errands at night. So she gave him a medal and taught him that it would protect him.

Bad religion gives him faith in the medal. Good religion gets him to see that ghosts do not exist.

The Guru's Cat

When the guru sat down to worship each evening the ashram cat would get in the way and distract the worshipers. So he ordered that the cat be tied during evening worship.

After the guru died the cat continued to be tied during evening worship. And when the cat expired, another cat was brought to the ashram so that it could be duly tied during evening worship.

Centuries later learned treatises were written by the guru's scholarly disciples on the liturgical significance of tying up a cat while worship is performed.

Don't Change

I was a neurotic for years. I was anxious and depressed and selfish. Everyone kept telling me to change.

I resented them, and I agreed with them, and I wanted to change, but simply couldn't, no matter how hard I tried.

What hurt the most was that, like the others, my best friend kept insisting that I change. So I felt powerless and trapped.

Then, one day, he said to me, "Don't change. I love you just as you are."

Those words were music to my ears: "Don't change. Don't change. Don't change...I love you as you are."

I relaxed. I came alive. And suddenly I changed!

Now I know that I couldn't really change until I found someone who would love me whether I changed or not.

Is this how you love me, God?

My Friend

Malik, son of Dinar, was much upset about the profligate behavior of a youth who lived next door to him. For a long time he took no action, hoping that someone else would intervene. But when the youth's behavior became intolerable Malik went to him and insisted that he change his ways.

The youth calmly replied that he was a protégé of the sultan and so nobody could prevent him from living the way he wanted.

Said Malik, "I shall personally complain to the sultan."

Said the youth, "That will be quite useless, because the sultan will never change his mind about me."

"I shall then denounce you to Allah," said Malik.

"Allah," said the youth, "is far too forgiving to condemn me."

Malik went away defeated. But after a while the youth's reputation became so bad that there was a public outcry about it. Malik decided it was his duty to attempt to reprimand him. As he was walking to the youth's house, however, he heard a voice say to him, "Do not touch my friend. He is under my protection." Malik was thrown into confusion by this and, when he was in the presence of the youth, did not know what to say.

Said the young man, "What have you come for now?"

Said Malik, "I came to reprimand you. But on my way here a voice told me not to touch you, for you are under his protection."

The profligate seemed stunned. "Did he call me his friend?" he asked. But by then Malik had already left his house. Years later Malik met this man in Mecca. He had been so touched by the words of the voice that he had given up his possessions and become a wandering beggar. "I have come here in search of my Friend," he said to Malik, and died.

God, the friend of a sinner! A statement as dangerous as it is effective. I tried it on myself once. I said, "God is far too forgiving to condemn me." And I suddenly heard the Good News — for the first time in my life.

The Job

Enter first applicant.

"You understand that this is a simple test we are giving you before we offer you the job you have applied for?"

"Yes."

"Well, what is two plus two?"

"Four."

Enter second applicant.

"Are you ready for the test?"

"Yes."

"Well, what is two plus two?"

"Whatever the boss says it is."

The second applicant got the job.

Which comes first, orthodoxy or the truth?

The Golden Eagle

A man found an eagle's egg and put it in the nest of a backyard hen. The eaglet hatched with the brood of chicks and grew up with them.

All his life the eagle did what the backyard chickens did, thinking he was a backyard chicken. He scratched the earth for worms and insects. He clucked and cackled. And he would thrash his wings and fly a few feet into the air.

Years passed and the eagle grew very old. One day he saw a magnificent bird far above him in the cloudless sky. It glided in graceful majesty among the powerful wind currents, with scarcely a beat of its strong golden wings.

The old eagle looked up in awe. "Who's that?" he asked.

"That's the eagle, the king of the birds," said his neighbor. "He belongs to the sky. We belong to the earth — we're chickens."

So the eagle lived and died a chicken, for that's what he thought he was.

Who Am I?

A tale from Attar of Nishapur:

The lover knocked at the door of his beloved. "Who knocks?" said the beloved from within.

"It is I," said the lover.

"Go away. This house will not hold you and me."

The rejected lover went into the desert. There he meditated for months on end, pondering the words of the beloved. Finally he returned and knocked at the door again.

"Who knocks?"

"It is you."

The door was immediately opened.

The Look of Jesus

In the Gospel according to Luke we read:

> But Peter said, "Man, I do not know what you are talking about." At that moment, while he was still speaking, a cock crew; and the Lord turned and looked straight at Peter . . . and Peter went outside and wept bitterly.

I had a fairly good relationship with the Lord. I would ask him for things, converse with him, praise him, thank him. . . .

But always I had this uncomfortable feeling that he wanted me to look at him. And I would not. I would talk, but look away when I sensed he was looking at me.

I was afraid I should find an accusation there of some un-repented sin. I thought I should find a demand there; there would be something he wanted from me.

One day I finally summoned up courage and looked! There was no accusation. There was no demand. The eyes just said, "I love you."

And I walked out and, like Peter, I wept.

Hafez Hayyim

In the last century, a tourist from the States visited the famous Polish rabbi Hafez Hayyim.

He was astonished to see that the rabbi's home was only a simple room filled with books. The only furniture was a table and a bench.

"Rabbi, where is your furniture?" asked the tourist.

"Where is yours?" replied Hafez.

"Mine? But I'm only a visitor here."

"So am I," said the rabbi.

The Diamond

The sannyasi had reached the outskirts of the village and settled down under a tree for the night when a villager came run-ning up to him and said, "The stone! The stone! Give me the precious stone!"

"What stone?" asked the sannyasi.

"Last night the Lord Shiva appeared to me in a dream," said the villager, "and told me that if I went to the outskirts of the village at dusk I should find a sannyasi who would give me a precious stone that would make me rich forever."

The sannyasi rummaged in his bag and pulled out a stone. "He probably meant this one," he said, as he handed the stone over to the villager. "I found it on a forest path some days ago. You can certainly have it."

The man gazed at the stone in wonder. It was a diamond, probably the largest diamond in the whole world, for it was as large as a person's head.

He took the diamond and walked away. All night he tossed about in bed, unable to sleep. Next day at the crack of dawn he woke the sannyasi and said, "Give me the wealth that makes it possible for you to give this diamond away so easily."

Religious Hatred

A tourist says to his guide, "You have a right to be proud of your town. I was especially impressed with the number of churches in it. Surely the people here must love the Lord."

"Well," replied the cynical guide, "They may love the Lord, but they sure as hell hate each other."

Like the little girl who, when asked, "Who are pagans?" replied, "Pagans are people who do not quarrel about religion."

The Singer's Voice Fills the Hall

Overheard outside a concert hall:

"What a singer! His voice filled the hall."

"Yes, several of us had to leave the hall to make room for it!"

Overheard in a spiritual counseling session:

"How can I love God as the scriptures tell us to? How can I give him my whole heart?"

"You must first empty your heart of all created things."

Misleading! Don't be afraid to fill your heart with the people and things you love, for the love of God won't occupy space in your heart any more than a singer's voice occupies space in a concert hall.

Love is not like a loaf of bread. If I give a chunk of the loaf to you I have less to offer to others. Love is like eucharistic bread: I receive the whole Christ. You receive the whole Christ too; and so does the next person, and the next.

You can love your mother with your whole heart, and your husband or wife, and each of your children. The wonder is that giving the whole of it to one person does not force you to give less to another. On the contrary, each one of them now gets more. For if you love only your friend and no one else it is a feeble heart that you offer. Your friend would stand to gain if you also gave it to others.

Thanks and Yes

What does it mean to *love* God? One does not love him the way one loves the people one sees and hears and touches, for God is not a *person* in our sense of the word. He is the Unknown. He is the wholly Other. He is above terms like "he" and "she," "person" and "thing."

When we say an audience fills the hall and a singer's voice fills the hall, we use the same word to refer to two totally distinct realities. When we say we love God with our whole heart and we love our friend with our whole heart, we also use the same words to express two totally distinct realities. The singer's voice does not really *fill* the hall. And we cannot really *love* God in the usual sense of the word.

To love God with one's whole heart means to say a wholehearted yes to life and all that life brings with it. To accept, without reservations, all that God has ordained for one's life. To have the attitude that Jesus had when he said, "Not my will, but yours be done." To love God with one's whole heart is to make one's own the words made famous by Dag Hammarskjöld:

> For all that has been, Thanks.
> To all that shall be, Yes.

This is the kind of thing one can give to God alone. In this he has no rivals. To understand that this is what it means to love God is to see at once that it doesn't come in the way of your loving your friends wholeheartedly, tenderly, passionately.

The singer's voice remains in undisputed possession of the hall, no matter how packed the hall is with people. Those people are no rival to it. The only rival is a person or a thing that causes you to weaken your attitude of *Yes* and *Thanks*.

3

Wellsprings
Spiritual Exercises

These exercises have a power that will not be experienced if they are merely read. They must be done. This is true of almost every sentence in an exercise. Often what seems to be an uninspiring set of words when read may prove to be, surprisingly, a gateway to enlightenment when done....

This book is meant to lead from mind to sense, from thought to fantasy and feeling — then, I hope, through feeling, fantasy, and sense to silence. So use it like a staircase to get up to the terrace. Once there, be sure to leave the stairs, or you will not see the sky.

When you are brought to silence this book will be your enemy. Get rid of it.

The Stranger

When the Messiah came
his people failed to see him.
He's still around.
When did I see him last?

I think of instances of love I gave
and got.

That was when God became incarnate once again.
Each time that knowledge liberated me
and set me free.
God's word was being revealed again.

The Prophet's burning gaze laid bare our sin
each time my heart flared up
at oppression and injustice,
each time my hidden depths were lit up in a flash
and my defenses were exposed.

At every inner healing I experienced
the Christ reached out and touched me.

And when I felt frustration, darkness, pain,
he struggled in his passion.

The inspiration felt
when I listened to a speech
or read a book
or watched a movie
was the Master calling to discipleship.

And in my prayerful silences
was not the Priest Supreme
uniting God and me?

I searched the recent past
to identify these grace-filled moments
and ask that he will come again today.

Then I imagine God anoints me as messiah
and I see myself fulfill this role
in each event that will take place today.

The Darkness

I think of myself as quite a decent person, good-hearted and
respected, with minor sins and failings, until it dawns on me
that the greatest sinners are the ones who sin in ignorance.

I see the well-intentioned damage
"love" inflicts on helpless children.

I see the marks of cruelty
in fervently religious people.
I see fair-minded Pharisees
assess the evidence against Jesus,
and consider it their duty to do away with him.

It frightens me
that I may be suffering from the sickness
of the chief priests and the Pharisees.

They were so certain of themselves,
so convinced that they were right,
so closed to other viewpoints and to change.
I think of people whom I know to be like that.
And then I think of me.

The Pharisees were given to judging.
People to them were either good or bad.
There was never any good in someone
who their prejudice said was bad.

I think of other people who seem to be like that.
I think of me.
I make a list of "bad" people I know
and wonder if at heart they might not be
far better than I am.

The Pharisees were men of the establishment.
They feared to rock the boat.
I think of me.

The Pharisees loved power.
They would force you to be good for your own sake.
They could not leave you free.
Again I think of me.

Finally, the Pharisee conformed.
He might see the accused before him as not being guilty
but he lacked the holy daring
to stand up to his peers and speak his mind.
I think, regretfully, of my fear to give offense,
to disagree,
my need to please.

I am no great improvement
on the men who killed the Savior.
All I can say is, "Lord, I am a sinner.
Be merciful to me."

I hear him answer gently,
"You are precious to my heart, my child."
Whatever could he mean by that?

I use his eyes to find out what he sees in me
that, even while he knows my sinfulness,
he says, "You are precious to my heart."

With those same eyes I look at "sinners"
— the Hitlers and the Stalins of our times.

I look at people I dislike ... reject.

Maybe I need those eyes of his
to bring me to compassion
and save me from the Pharisee in me.

The Hazard

I recall the words of Paul,
"Let this mind be in you
which was in Jesus Christ."

I ask the Lord to offer me his heart.
I see him take away my heart of stone,
put in its place his heart of flesh.

I feel the strange sensation
of returning to my world
with someone else's heart.

I sense in me an urge to pray.
I hurry to my usual place of prayer
and feel my new heart doing unusual things.

I walk along a busy street.
The usual crowds are everywhere
and I look at them, to my astonishment,
in a strangely different kind of way today.
The sight of them awakens thoughts and feelings
quite different from the ones I am accustomed to.

I set out for my home
and as I walk I look at trees and birds,
at clouds and animals and all of nature
with a different kind of vision.

At home,
at work,
I look at people I dislike
and see myself reacting differently.
The same thing happens
with the people to whom I formerly felt neutral.
And realize, to my surprise, that I am different
even with the ones I love.

I notice that with this new heart of mine
I am strong in situations
that I formerly avoided.

There are occasions
when my heart dissolves in tenderness
and others when it burns with indignation.

My new heart makes me independent:
I do not cease to be attached to many things,
but the clinging disappears

—I feel free to let them go.
I try this out delightedly,
moving from one attachment to another.

Then, to my alarm, it steers me into situations
that get me into trouble.
I find myself involved in things
that put an end to my desire for comfort.
I say things that antagonize.

Finally I come back to the presence of the Lord
to give him back his heart.
It was exciting to be fitted
with the heart of Christ himself.

But I know I am not ready for it yet.
I still need to protect myself a little.

But even as I take my poor heart back
I know that I will be a different person
from having felt, if only for a moment,
what it meant to have this heart, this mind in me
that was in Jesus Christ our Lord.

The King

Moments after Jesus has died I stand on the hill of Calvary,
unconscious of the crowd. It is as if I am alone, my eyes fixed
on that lifeless body on the cross.

I watch the thoughts and feelings
that arise within me as I look.

I see the crucified as stripped of everything:

Stripped of his dignity,
naked before his friends and enemies.

Stripped of his reputation.
My mind goes back to scenes and times

when he was spoken well of.
Stripped of success.
I recall the heady years
when his miracles were acclaimed
and it seemed as if the Kingdom
were about to be established.

Stripped of credibility.
So he could not come down from the cross.
So he could not save himself
—he must have been a fraud.

Stripped of support.
Even the friends who did not run away
are powerless to reach him.

Stripped of his God
—the God he thought of as his Father,
who he hoped would save him in his hour of need.

Finally I see him stripped of life,
this existence here on earth
that he, like us, held on to tenaciously
and was unwilling to let go of.

As I gaze at that lifeless body I slowly understand
that I am looking at the symbol
of supreme and total liberation.
In being fastened to the cross
Jesus becomes alive and free.
Here is a parable of conquest, not defeat.
It calls for envy, not commiseration.

So now I contemplate the majesty of the man
who has freed himself
from all that makes us slaves,
destroys our happiness.

In gazing at that freedom
I think with sadness of my slavery.

I am a slave to public opinion.
I think of the times I am controlled
by what society will say and think of me.

I am driven to success.
I see the times I run away from challenges and risks
— because I hate to make mistakes or fail.

I am enslaved by the need for human consolation:
How many times I was dependent
on the approval and acceptance of my friends
and their power to assuage my loneliness...
the times I was possessive of my friends
and lost my freedom.

I think of my enslavement to my God.
I think of the times I try to use him
to make my life secure
and undisturbed and painless.
Also the times I am enslaved by fear of him
and by the need to protect myself against him
through rites and superstitions.

Finally I think of how I cling to life,
how paralyzed I am by fears of every kind,
unable to take risks
for fear of losing friends or reputation,
success or life or God.

And so I gaze in admiration at the crucified
who won his final liberation in his passion
when he fought with his attachments,
let go of them,
and conquered.

I see the lines of people everywhere
who will kneel today, Good Friday,
in adoration of the crucified.
I perform my adoration here on Calvary,

completely unaware of the noisy crowd around me:
I kneel and touch my forehead to the ground,
desiring for myself
the freedom and the victory
that shine out in that body on the cross.

And in my adoration
I hear those haunting words re-echo in my heart:
"If you wish to follow me,
you must follow with your cross."
And those other words, "Unless it dies,
the grain of wheat remains alone."

The Exposure

I think of the times I come alive
and the times when I am dead.

I ponder on the features I assume
in moments of aliveness
and in times when I am dead.

Life abhors security:
for life means taking risks,
exposing self to danger,
even death.
Jesus says that those who wish to be safe will lose their
    lives;
those who are prepared to lose their lives will keep them.

I think of the times
when I drew back from taking risks,
when I was comfortable and safe;
those were times when I stagnated.

I think of other times
when I dared to take a chance,
to make mistakes,
to be a failure

and a fool,
to be criticized by others,
when I dared to risk being hurt
and to cause pain to others.
I was alive!

Life is for the gambler.
The coward dies.

Life is at variance with my perception
of what is good and bad:
these things are good and to be sought;
these others bad and to be shunned.
To eat of the Tree of Knowing Good and Bad
is to fall from paradise.
I must learn to accept whatever life may bring,
pleasure and pain, sorrow and joy.
For if I close myself to pain
my capacity for pleasure dies
—I harden myself
and repress what I regard as unpleasant and undesirable,
and in that hardness, that repression,
is rigidity and death.

So I decide to taste in all its fullness
the experience of the present moment,
calling no experience good or bad.
Those experiences that I dread—I think of them,
and, inasmuch as I am able, I let them come
and stop resisting them.

Life goes hand in hand with change.
What does not change is dead.
I think of people who are fossils.
I think of times when I was fossilized:
no change, no newness,
the same old worn-out concepts
and patterns of behavior,

the same mentality, neuroses,
habits, prejudices.

Dead people have a built-in fear of change.
What changes have there been in me
over the past six months?
What changes will there be today?

I end this exercise
by watching nature all around me:
so flexible,
so flowing,
so fragile,
insecure,
exposed to death
—and so alive!

The Liberation

Become conscious of your body as a whole
and of the sensations you experience
in its various parts.

Now turn your attention
to the one who has been watching
the sensations and the body.

Realize that the observer, the "I,"
is not the same as the sensations
that are being observed.

You may explicitly say to yourself,
"I am not these sensations.
I am not this body."

Now become conscious of your breathing.

Then turn your attention
to the one who has been looking
at the breathing.

Realize that the observer, the "I,"
is different from the breathing
that is being observed.

You may explicitly say to yourself,
"I am not the breathing."

Become conscious of every thought
that you are thinking.
It is quite likely
that soon all thoughts will disappear
and all you will be conscious of is this one thought:
right-now-there-is-no-thinking-in-my-mind.

Turn your attention now
to the one who is attending to those thoughts
or the one who is producing them.

Realize that the observing, the "I,"
is different from the thoughts observed.

You may explicitly say to yourself,
"I am not the thoughts.
I am not the thinking."

Observe a feeling
that you are now experiencing
— or recall one you have had before —
particularly if it is a negative emotion
like fear, anxiety, hurt, discouragement, remorse.

Turn your attention
to the one who has been watching
— or recalling — the emotion.

Realize that the observer, the "I,"
is different from the feeling
that is being observed.

You may explicitly say to yourself,
"I am not the feeling."

4

One Minute Wisdom

"Is there such a thing as One Minute Wisdom?"
  "There certainly is," said the master.
  "But surely one minute is too brief?"
  "It is fifty-nine seconds too long."
  To his puzzled disciples the master later said, "How much time does it take to catch sight of the moon?"
  "Then why all these years of spiritual endeavor?"
  "Opening one's eyes may take a lifetime. Seeing is done in a flash."

The master in these tales is not a single person. He is a Hindu guru, a Zen roshi, a Taoist sage, a Jewish rabbi, a Christian monk, a Sufi mystic. He is Lao-tzu and Socrates. Buddha and Jesus, Zarathustra and Mohammed. His teaching is found in the seventh century B.C.E. and the twentieth century C.E. His wisdom belongs to East and West alike. Do his historical antecedents really matter? History, after all, is the record of appearances, not Reality; of doctrines, not Silence.

It will only take a minute to read each of the anecdotes that follow. You will probably find the master's language baffling, exasperating, even downright meaningless. This, alas, is not an easy book! It was written not to instruct but to Awaken. Concealed within its pages (not in the printed words, not even in the tales, but in its spirit, its moods, its atmosphere) is a Wisdom which cannot be conveyed in human speech. As you read the printed pages and struggle with the master's cryptic language, it is possible that you will unwittingly chance upon the Silent Teaching that lurks within the book, and be Awakened — and transformed. This is what Wisdom means: to be changed without the slightest effort on your part, to be transformed, believe it or not, merely by waking to the reality that is not words, that lies beyond the reach of words.

If you are fortunate enough to be Awakened thus, you will know why the finest language is the one that is not spoken, the finest action is the one that is not done and the finest change is the one that is not willed.

Caution: Take the tales in tiny doses — one or two at a time. An overdose will lower their potency.

Myths

The master gave his teaching in parables and stories, which his disciples listened to with pleasure — and occasional frustration, for they longed for something deeper.

The master was unmoved. To all their objections he would say, "You have yet to understand, my dears, that the shortest distance between a human being and truth is a story."

Another time he said, "Do not despise the story. A lost gold coin is found by means of a penny candle; the deepest truth is found by means of a simple story."

Miracles

A man traversed land and sea to check for himself the master's extraordinary fame.

"What miracles has your master worked?" he said to a disciple.

"Well, there are miracles and miracles. In your land it is regarded as a miracle if God does someone's will. In our country it is regarded as a miracle if someone does the will of God."

Identity

"How does one seek union with God?"

"The harder you seek, the more distance you create between Him and you."

"So what does one do about the distance?"

"Understand that it isn't there."

"Does that mean that God and I are one?"

"Not one. Not two."

"How is that possible?"

"The sun and its light, the ocean and the wave, the singer and his song — not one. Not two."

Worship

To the disciple who was overly respectful the master said, "Light is reflected on a wall. Why venerate the wall? Be attentive to the light."

Destiny

To a woman who complained about her destiny the master said, "It is you who make your destiny."

"But surely I am not responsible for being born a woman?"

"Being born a woman isn't destiny. That is fate. Destiny is how you accept your womanhood and what you make of it."

Discrimination

Said the jilted lover, "I have burned my fingers once. I shall never fall in love again."

Said the master, "You are like the cat who, having burned itself from sitting on a stove, refused to sit again."

Philosophy

Before the visitor embarked upon discipleship, he wanted assurance from the master.

"Can you teach me the goal of human life?"

"I cannot."

"Or at least its meaning?"

"I cannot."

"Can you indicate to me the nature of death and of life beyond the grave?"

"I cannot."

The visitor walked away in scorn. The disciples were dismayed that their master had been shown up in a poor light.

Said the master soothingly, "Of what is it to comprehend life's nature and life's meaning if you have never tasted it? I'd rather you ate your pudding than speculated on it."

Rebirth

"Make a clean break with your past and you will be Enlightened," said the master.

"I am doing that by degrees."

"Growth is achieved by degrees. Enlightenment is instantaneous."

Later he said, "Take the leap! You cannot cross a chasm in little jumps."

Atheism

To the disciples' delight the master said he wanted a new shirt for his birthday. The finest cloth was brought. The village tailor came in to have the master measured, and promised, by the will of God, to make the shirt within a week.

A week went by and a disciple was dispatched to the tailor

while the master excitedly waited for his shirt. Said the tailor, "There has been a slight delay. But, by the will of God, it will be ready by tomorrow."

Next day the tailor said, "I'm sorry it isn't done. Try again tomorrow and, if God so wills, it will certainly be ready."

The following day the master said, "Ask him how long it will take if he keeps God out of it."

Transformation

To a disciple who was forever complaining about others the master said, "If it is peace you want, seek to change yourself, not other people. It is easier to protect your feet with slippers than to carpet the whole of the earth."

Distinction

The master was strolling with some of his disciples along the bank of a river.

He said, "See how the fish keep darting about wherever they please. That's what they really enjoy."

A stranger overhearing that remark said, "How do you know what fish enjoy? You're not a fish."

The disciples gasped at what they took for impudence. The master smiled at what he recognized as a fearless spirit of inquiry.

He replied affably, "And you, my friend, how do you know I am not a fish? You are not I."

The disciples laughed, taking this to be a well-deserved rebuff. Only the stranger was struck by its depth.

All day he pondered it, then came to the monastery to say, "Maybe you are not as different from the fish as I thought. Or I from you."

Authenticity

The master was never impressed by diplomas or degrees. He scrutinized the person, not the certificate.

He was once heard to say, "When you have ears to hear a bird in song, you don't need to look at its credentials."

Love

A newly married couple said, "What shall we do to make our love endure?"

Said the master, "Love other things together."

Flow

When it became clear that the master was going to die, the disciples were depressed.

Said the master smilingly, "Don't you see that death gives loveliness to life?"

"No. We'd much rather you never died."

"Whatever is truly alive must die. Look at the flowers; only plastic flowers never die."

Riches

"How would spirituality help a man of the world like me?" said the businessman.

"It will help you to have more," said the master.

"How?"

"By teaching you to desire less."

Nature

A lecturer explained how a fraction of the enormous sums spent on arms in the modern world would solve all the material problems of every member of the human race.

The inevitable reaction of the disciples after the lecture was: "But why are human beings so stupid?"

"Because," said the master solemnly, "People have learned to read printed books. They have forgotten the art of reading unprinted ones."

"Give us an example of an unprinted book."

But the master wouldn't give one.

One day, in response to their persistence, he said: "The songs of birds, the sounds of insects are all trumpeting forth the truth. The grasses and the flowers are all pointing out the Way. Listen! Look! That is the way to read!"

Heaven

To a disciple who was obsessed with the thought of life after death the master said, "Why waste a single moment thinking of the hereafter?"

"But is it possible not to?"

"Yes."

"How?"

"By living in heaven here and now."

"And where is this heaven?"

"In the here and now."

Noninstruction

"What does your master teach?" asked a visitor.

"Nothing," said the disciple.

"Then why does he give discourses?"

"He only points the way — he teaches nothing."

The visitor couldn't make sense out of this, so the disciple made it clearer: "If the master were to teach we would make beliefs out of his teachings. The master is not concerned with what we believe — only with what we see."

Appearances

The master always frowned on anything that seemed sensational. "The divine," he claimed, "is only found in the ordinary."

To a disciple who was attempting forms of asceticism that bordered on the bizarre the master was heard to say, "Holiness is a mysterious thing: The greater it is, the less it is noticed."

Words

The disciples were absorbed in a discussion of Lao-tzu's dictum:

> Those who know do not say;
> Those who say do not know.

When the master entered, they asked him exactly what the words meant.

Said the master, "Which of you knows the fragrance of a rose?"

All of them knew.

Then he said, "Put it into words."

All of them were silent.

Discipline

To the disciples who wanted to know what sort of meditation he practiced each morning in the garden the master said, "When I look carefully, I see the rose bush in full bloom."

"Why would one have to look *carefully* to see the rose bush?" they asked.

"Lest one see not the rose bush," said the master, "but one's preconception of it."

Unobtrusiveness

A man of spiritual repute came to the master and said, "I cannot pray, I cannot understand the scriptures, I cannot do the exercises that I prescribe to others...."

"Then give it all up," said the master cheerfully.

"But how can I? I am supposed to be a holy man and have a following in these parts."

Later the master said with a sigh: "Holiness today is a name without a reality. It is only genuine when it is a reality without a name."

Humility

To a visitor who described himself as a seeker after truth the master said, "If what you seek is truth, there is one thing you must have above all else."

"I know. An overwhelming passion for it."

"No. An unremitting readiness to admit you may be wrong."

At-one-ment

When a man whose marriage was in trouble sought his advice, the master said, "You must learn to listen to your wife."

The man took this advice to heart and returned after a month to say that he had learned to listen to every word his wife was saying.

Said the master with a smile, "Now go home and listen to every word she isn't saying."

Tribulation

"Calamities can bring growth and Enlightenment," said the master.

And he explained it thus: "Each day a bird would shelter in the withered branches of a tree that stood in the middle of a vast deserted plain. One day a whirlwind uprooted the tree, forcing the poor bird to fly a hundred miles in search of shelter — till it finally came to a forest of fruit-laden trees."

And he concluded: "If the withered tree had survived, nothing would have induced the bird to give up its security and fly."

Incompetence

The master would insist that the final barrier to our attaining God was the word and concept "God."

This so infuriated the local priest that he came in a huff to argue the matter out with the master.

"But surely the word 'God' can lead us to God?" said the priest.

"It can," said the master calmly.

"How can something help and be a barrier?"

Said the master, "The donkey that brings you to the door is not the means by which you enter the house."

Art

"Of what use is a master?" someone asked.

Said the disciple, "To teach you what you have always known, to show you what you are always looking at."

When this confused the visitor, the disciple exclaimed: "An artist, by his paintings, taught me to see the sunset. The master, by his teachings, taught me to see the reality of every moment."

Affirmation

A woman in great distress over the death of her son came to the master for comfort.

He listened to her patiently while she poured out her tale of woe.

Then he said softly, "I cannot wipe away your tears, my dear. I can only teach you how to make them holy."

Disclosure

The discussion among the disciples once centered on the usefulness of reading. Some thought it was a waste of time, others disagreed.

When the master was appealed to, he said, "Have you ever read one of those texts in which the notes scrawled in the margin by a reader prove to be as illuminating as the text itself?"

The disciples nodded in agreement.

"Life," said the master, "is one such text."

Wisdom

It always pleased the master to hear people recognize their ignorance.

"Wisdom tends to grow in proportion to one's awareness of one's ignorance," he claimed.

When asked for an explanation, he said, "When you come to see you are not as wise today as you thought you were yesterday, you are wiser today."

Thought

"Why are you so wary of thought?" said the philosopher. "Thought is the one tool we have for organizing the world."

"True. But thought can organize the world so well that you are no longer able to see it."

To his disciples he later said, "A thought is a screen, not a mirror; that is why you live in a thought envelope, untouched by Reality."

Restriction

The master was exceedingly gracious to university dons who visited him, but he would never reply to their questions or be drawn into their theological speculations.

To his disciples, who marveled at this, he said, "Can one talk about the ocean to a frog in a well — or about the divine to people who are restricted by their concepts?"

Totalitarianism

To the disciples' embarrassment the master once told a bishop that religious people have a natural bent for cruelty.

"Why?" demanded the disciples after the bishop had gone.

"Because they all too easily sacrifice persons for the advancement of a purpose," said the master.

Recognition

As the master grew old and infirm, the disciples begged him not to die. Said the master, "If I did not go, how would you ever see?"

"What is it we fail to see when you are with us?" they asked.

But the master would not say.

When the moment of his death was near, they said, "What is it we will see when you are gone?"

With a twinkle in his eye, the master said, "All I did was sit on the riverbank handing out river water. After I'm gone, I trust you will notice the river."

Escape

The master became a legend in his lifetime. It was said that God once sought his advice: "I want to play a game of hide-and-seek with humankind. I've asked my angels what the best place is to hide in. Some say the depth of the ocean. Others the top of the highest mountain. Others still the far side of the moon or a distant star. What do you suggest?"

Said the master, "Hide in the human heart. That's the last place they will think of!"

5

Taking Flight
Story Meditations

Warning

It is a great mystery that though the human heart longs for
Truth, in which alone it finds liberation and delight, the first
reaction of human beings to Truth is one of hostility and fear.
So the Spiritual Teachers of humanity, like Buddha and Jesus,
created a device to circumvent the opposition of their listeners:
the story. They knew that the most entrancing words a language
holds are "Once upon a time . . . ," that it is common to oppose
a truth but impossible to resist a story. Vyasa, the author of the
Mahabharata, says that if you listen carefully to a story you will
never be the same again. That is because the story will worm
its way into your heart and break down barriers to the divine.
Even if you read the stories in this book only for the entertainment there is no guarantee that an occasional story will not slip
through your defenses and explode when you least expect it to.
So you have been warned!

   If you are foolhardy enough to court enlightenment, this is
what I suggest you do:

   A. Carry a story around in your mind so you can dwell on
it in leisure moments. That will give it a chance to work on
your subconscious and reveal its hidden meaning. You will then

be surprised to see how it comes to you quite unexpectedly just when you need it to light up an event or situation and bring you insight and inner healing. That is when you will realize that, in exposing yourself to these stories, you were auditing a Course in Enlightenment for which no guru is needed other than yourself!

B. Since each of these stories is a revelation of Truth, and since Truth, when spelled with a capital *T*, means the truth about you, make sure that each time you read a story you single-mindedly search for a deeper understanding of yourself. Read it the way one would read a medical book — wondering if one has any of the symptoms; and not a psychology book — thinking what typical specimens one's friends are. If you succumb to the temptation of seeking insight into others, the stories will do you damage.

•

So passionate was Mullah Nasruddin's love for truth that he traveled to distant places in search of Koranic scholars and he felt no inhibitions about drawing infidels at the bazaar into discussions about the truths of his faith. One day his wife told him how unfairly he was treating her — and discovered that her husband had no interest whatsoever in that kind of Truth!

It's the only kind that matters, of course. Ours would be a different world, indeed, if those of us who are scholars and ideologues, whether religious or secular, had the same passion for self-knowledge that we display for our theories and dogmas.

•

There was once a woman who was religious and devout and filled with love for God. Each morning she would go to church. And on her way children would call out to her, beggars would accost her, but so immersed was she in her devotions that she did not even see them.

Now one day she walked down the street in her customary manner and arrived at the church just in time for service.

She pushed the door, but it would not open. She pushed it again harder, and found the door was locked. Distressed at the thought that she would miss service for the first time in years and not knowing what to do, she looked up. And there, right before her face, she found a note pinned to the door.

It said, "I'm out there!"

•

When Brother Bruno was at prayer one night, he was disturbed by the croaking of a bullfrog. All his attempts to disregard the sound were unsuccessful, so he shouted from his window, "Quiet! I'm at my prayers."

Now Brother Bruno was a saint, so his command was instantly obeyed. Every living creature held its voice so as to create a silence that would be favorable to prayer.

But now another sound intruded on Bruno's worship — an inner voice that said, "Maybe God is as pleased with the croaking of that frog as with the chanting of your psalms."

"What can please the ears of God in the croak of a frog?" was Bruno's scornful rejoinder.

But the voice refused to give up. "Why would you think God invented the sound?"

Bruno decided to find out why. He leaned out of his window and gave the order, "Sing!" The bullfrog's measured croaking filled the air to the ludicrous accompaniment of all the frogs in the vicinity. And as Bruno attended to the sound, their voices ceased to jar, for he discovered that, if he stopped resisting them, they actually enriched the silence of the night.

With that discovery Bruno's heart became harmonious with the universe, and, for the first time in his life, he understood what it means to pray.

•

Once the master was at prayer. The disciples came up to him and said, "Sir, teach us how to pray." This is how he taught them. . . .

Two men were once walking through a field when they saw an angry bull. Instantly they made for the nearest fence with the bull in hot pursuit. It soon became evident to them that they were not going to make it, so one man shouted to the other, "We've had it! Nothing can save us. Say a prayer. Quick!"

The other shouted back, "I've never prayed in my life, and I don't have a prayer for this occasion."

"Never mind. The bull is catching up with us. Any prayer will do."

"Well, I'll say the one I remember my father used to say before meals: 'For what we are about to receive, Lord, make us truly grateful.'"

Nothing surpasses the holiness of those who have learned perfect acceptance of everything that is.

In the game of cards called life one plays the hand one is dealt to the best of one's ability.

Those who insist on playing not the hand they were given, but the one they insist they should have been dealt — these are life's failures.

We are not asked if we will play. That is not an option. Play we must. The option is how.

•

A man got into a bus and found himself sitting next to a youngster who was obviously a hippie. He was wearing only one shoe.

"You've evidently lost a shoe, son."

"No, man," came the reply. "I found one."

It is evident to me; that does not mean it is true.

•

A man took his new hunting dog out on a trial hunt. Presently he shot a duck that fell into the lake. The dog walked over the water, picked up the duck, and brought it to his master.

The man was flabbergasted! He shot another duck. Once again, while he rubbed his eyes in disbelief, the dog walked over the water and retrieved the duck.

Hardly daring to believe what he had seen, he called his neighbor for a shoot the following day. Once again, each time he or his neighbor hit a bird, the dog would walk over the water and bring the bird in. The man said nothing. Neither did his neighbor. Finally, unable to contain himself any longer, he blurted out, "Did you notice anything strange about that dog?"

The neighbor rubbed his chin pensively. "Yes," he finally said. "Come to think of it, I did! The son of a gun can't swim!"

It isn't as if life is not full of miracles. It's more than that: It is miraculous, and anyone who stops taking it for granted will see it at once.

•

Two brothers — one a bachelor, the other married — owned a farm whose fertile soil yielded an abundance of grain. Half the grain went to one brother and half to the other.

All went well at first. Then, every now and then, the married man began to wake with a start from his sleep at night and think: "This isn't fair. My brother isn't married, he's all alone, and he gets only half the produce of the farm. Here I am with a wife and five kids, so I have all the security I need for my old age. But who will care for my poor brother when he gets old? He needs to save much more for the future than he does at present, so his need is obviously greater than mine."

With that he would get out of bed, steal over to his brother's place, and pour a sackful of grain into his brother's granary.

The bachelor brother too began to get the same attacks. Every once in a while he would wake from his sleep and say to himself: "This simply isn't fair. My brother has a wife and five kids and he gets only half the produce of the land. Now I have no one except myself to support. So is it just that my poor brother, whose need is obviously greater than mine, should re-

ceive exactly as much as I do?" Then he would get out of bed
and pour a sackful of grain into his brother's granary.

One night they got out of bed at the same time and ran into
each other, each with a sack of grain on his back!

Many years later, after their death, the story leaked out. So
when the townsfolk wanted to build a church, they chose the
spot at which the two brothers met, for they could not think of
any place in the town that was holier than that one.

The important religious distinction is not between those who
worship and those who do not worship but between those who
love and those who don't.

•

A drunk was staggering across a bridge one night when he ran
into a friend. The two of them leaned over the bridge and began
chatting for a while.

"What's that down there?" asked the drunk suddenly.

"That's the moon," said his friend.

The drunk looked again, shook his head in disbelief and said,
"Okay, okay. But how the hell did I get way up here?"

We almost never see reality. What we see is a reflection of it
in the form of words and concepts which we then proceed to
take for reality. The world we live in is mostly a mental con-
struct. People feed on words, live by words, would fall apart
without them.

•

DISCIPLE: What's the difference between knowledge and enlightenment?

MASTER: When you have knowledge, you use a torch to show
the way. When you are enlightened, you become a torch.

•

A group was enjoying the music at a Chinese restaurant. Suddenly a soloist struck up a vaguely familiar tune; everyone

recognized the melody, but no one could remember its name. So they beckoned to the splendidly clad waiter and asked him to find out what the musician was playing. The waiter waddled across the floor, then returned with a look of triumph on his face and declared in a loud whisper, "Violin!"

The scholar's contribution to spirituality!

•

There was once an ascetic who lived a celibate life and made it his life's mission to fight against sex in himself and others.

In due course he died. And his disciple, who could not stand the shock, died a little after him. When the disciple reached the other world he couldn't believe what he saw: There was his beloved master with the most extraordinarily beautiful woman seated on his lap!

His sense of shock faded when it occurred to him that his master was being rewarded for his sexual abstinence on earth. He went up to him and said, "Beloved Master, now I know that God is just, for you are being rewarded in heaven for your austerities on earth."

The master seemed annoyed. "Idiot!" he said, "This isn't heaven and I'm not being rewarded—she's being punished."

When the shoe fits, the foot is forgotten; when the belt fits, the waist is forgotten; when all things are in harmony, the ego is forgotten.

Of what use, then, are your austerities?

•

An old woman in the village was said to be receiving divine apparitions. The local priest demanded proof of their authenticity. "When God next appears to you," he said, "ask Him to tell you my sins, which are known to Him alone. That should be evidence enough."

The woman returned a month later and the priest asked if

God had appeared to her again. She said He had. "Did you put the question to Him?"

"I did."

"And what did He say?"

"He said, 'Tell your priest I have forgotten his sins.' "

Is it possible that all of the horrible things you have done have been forgotten by everyone — except yourself?

•

Soon after the death of Rabbi Mokshe, Rabbi Mendel of Kotyk asked one of his disciples, "What did your teacher give the greatest importance to?"

The disciple gave it a moment's reflection, then said, "To whatever he happened to be doing at the moment."

•

A guru asked his disciples how they could tell when the night had ended and the day begun.

One said, "When you see an animal in the distance and can tell whether it is a cow or a horse."

"No," said the guru.

"When you look at a tree in the distance and can tell if it is a neem tree or a mango tree."

"Wrong again," said the guru.

"Well, then, what is it?" asked his disciples.

"When you look into the face of any man and recognize your brother in him; when you look into the face of any woman and recognize in her your sister. If you cannot do this, no matter what time it is by the sun it is still night."

•

It intrigued the congregation to see their rabbi disappear each week on the eve of the Sabbath. They suspected he was secretly meeting the Almighty, so they deputed one of their number to follow him.

This is what the man saw: The rabbi disguised himself in peasant clothes and served a paralyzed Gentile woman in her cottage, cleaning out the room and preparing a Sabbath meal for her.

When the spy got back, the congregation asked, "Where did the rabbi go? Did he ascend to heaven?"

"No," the man replied, "he went even higher."

•

Truth is not found in formulas . . .

A man was drinking tea with a friend in a restaurant. He looked long and hard at his cup, and then said with a resigned sigh, "Ah, my friend, life is like a cup of tea."

The other pondered this for a while, looked long and hard at his own cup, and then asked, "Why? Why is life like a cup of tea?"

The man said, "How should I know? Am I an intellectual?"

•

. . . or in theories. . . .

A manager, who had just returned from a motivation seminar, called an employee into his office and said, "Henceforth you are going to be allowed to plan and control your job. That will raise productivity considerably, I am sure."

"Will I be paid more?" asked the worker.

"No, no. Money is not a motivator and you will get no satisfaction from a salary raise."

"Well, if production does increase, will I be paid more?"

"Look," said the manager. "You obviously do not understand the motivation theory. Take this book home and read it; it explains what it is that really motivates you."

As the man was leaving, he stopped and said, "If I read this book will I be paid more?"

•

...or in slogans...

A religious group was in the habit of using for its many conferences a hotel whose motto was written in large words over the walls of the lobby: THERE ARE NO PROBLEMS, ONLY OPPORTUNITIES.

A man approached the hotel desk and said, "Excuse me, I have a problem."

The desk clerk said with a smile, "We have no problems here, sir. Only opportunities."

"Call it what you want," said the man impatiently. "There's a woman in the room assigned to me."

•

...or in labels....

An Englishman emigrated to the United States and became an American citizen.

When he went back to England for a vacation, one of his relatives reprimanded him for changing his citizenship.

"What have you gained by becoming an American citizen?"

"Well, for one thing, I win the American Revolution," was the answer.

•

Nor is it generally found in statistics....

Nasruddin was arrested and taken to court on the charge that he was stuffing horse meat into the chicken cutlets he served at his restaurant.

Before passing sentence, the judge wanted to know in what proportion he was mixing the horse meat with chicken flesh. Nasruddin said, on oath, "It was fifty-fifty, Your Honor."

After the trial a friend asked what exactly "fifty-fifty" meant. Said Nasruddin, "One horse to one chicken."

•

It is concrete....

A monk once said to Fuketsu, "There is something I heard you say once that puzzled me, namely, that truth can be communicated without speaking and without keeping silent. Would you explain this please?"

Fuketsu replied, "When I was a lad in South China, ah! How the birds sang among the blossoms in the springtime!"

I think therefore I am unconscious.
At the moment of thought I dwell in the UNREAL world of abstraction, or of the past, or of the future.

•

It can be relative...

An American tourist was traveling abroad for the first time. On arrival at his first foreign airport he was faced with a choice between two passageways, one of which was marked CITIZENS and the other ALIENS.

He promptly headed for the first one. When told later that he would have to stand in the other line, he protested, "But I'm no alien. I'm an American!"

•

...and calls for that most formidable accomplishment of the human spirit — an open mind....

The story has it that when New Mexico became part of the United States and the first court session opened in the new state, the presiding judge was a hardened old former cowboy and Indian fighter.

He took his place on the bench and the case opened. A man was charged with horse stealing. The case for the prosecution was made; the plaintiff and his witnesses were duly heard.

Whereupon the attorney for the defendant stood up and said, "And now, Your Honor, I should like to present my client's side of the case."

Said the judge, "Sit down. That won't be necessary. It would only confuse the jury!"

If you have one watch, you know the time. If you have two watches, you're never sure.

6

The Heart of the Enlightened
Story Meditations

To succeed in the adventure called spirituality one must have one's mind set on getting the most out of life. Most people settle for trifles such as wealth, fame, comfort, and human company.

A man was so enamored of fame he was ready to hang on a gibbet if that would get his name in the headlines. Is there really a difference between him and most businesspeople and politicians? (Not to mention the rest of us who set such store by public opinion.)

•

The priest looked at him fiercely and said, "Don't you want to go to heaven?"

"No," said the man.

"Do you mean to stand there and tell me you don't want to go to heaven when you die?"

"Of course, I want to go to heaven when I die. I thought you were going now!"

We are ready to go all the way — only when our brakes don't work.

•

When the sparrow builds its nest in the forest, it occupies but a single branch. When the deer slakes its thirst at the river, it drinks no more than its belly can hold.

We collect things because our hearts are empty.

•

The guru sat in meditation on the riverbank when a disciple bent down to place two enormous pearls at his feet, a token of reverence and devotion.

The guru opened his eyes, lifted one of the pearls, and held it so carelessly that it slipped out of his hand and rolled down the bank into the river.

The horrified disciple plunged in after it, but though he dived in again and again till late evening, he had no luck.

Finally, all wet and exhausted, he roused the guru from his meditation: "You saw where it fell. Show me the spot so I can get it back for you."

The guru lifted the other pearl, threw it into the river, and said, "Right there!"

Do not attempt to possess things, for things cannot really be possessed. Only make sure you are not possessed by them and you will be the sovereign of creation.

•

A visitor to an insane asylum found one of the inmates rocking back and forth in a chair cooing repeatedly in a soft, contented manner, "Lulu, Lulu..."

"What's this man's problem?" he asked the doctor.

"Lulu. She was the woman who jilted him," was the doctor's reply.

As they proceeded on the tour, they came to a padded cell whose occupant was banging his head repeatedly against the wall and moaning, "Lulu, Lulu..."

"Is Lulu this man's problem too?" asked the visitor.

"Yes," said the doctor. "He is the one Lulu finally married."

There are only two afflictions in life: not getting what you are attached to and getting what you are attached to.

•

There was once a very austere man who let no food or drink pass his lips while the sun was in the heavens. In what seemed to be a sign of heavenly approval for his austerities, a bright star shone on top of a nearby mountain, visible to everyone in broad daylight, though no one knew what had brought the star there.

One day the man decided to climb the mountain. A little village girl insisted on going with him. The day was warm, and soon the two were thirsty. He urged the child to drink, but she said she would not unless he drank too. The poor man was in a quandary. He hated to break his fast; but he hated to see the child suffer from thirst. Finally, he drank. And the child with him.

For a long time he dared not to look up to the sky, for he feared the star had gone. So imagine his surprise when, on looking up after a while, he saw two stars shining brightly above the mountain.

•

A woman once came to Rabbi Israel and told him her secret sorrow: She had been married twenty years and still had not borne a son. "What a coincidence!" said the rabbi. "It was exactly thus with my mother." And this is the story he told her: For twenty years his mother had had no child. One day she heard that the holy Baal Shem Tov was in town, so she hurried to the house he was in and begged him to pray that she might have a son.

"What are you willing to do about it?" the holy man asked.

"What can I do?" she replied. "My husband is a poor librarian, but I do have something I can offer the rabbi." With that she rushed home, pulled a katinka out of the chest where it had been carefully stored away, and ran back again to offer it to the rabbi. Now the katinka, as everyone knows, was the cape worn by the bride on her wedding day — a precious heirloom handed down from one generation to another. By the time the woman got back, the rabbi had left for another town, so that is where she went. Being poor, however, she had to walk the distance; by the time she got there, the rabbi had left for another destination. Six weeks she followed after him from town to town till she finally caught up with him. The rabbi took the katinka and gave it to the local synagogue.

Then Rabbi Israel concluded, "My mother walked all the way back home. A year later I was born."

"What a coincidence, indeed!" cried the woman. "I, too, have a katinka at home. I shall bring it to you at once, and if you offer it to the local synagogue, God will give me a son."

"Ah no, my dear," said the rabbi sadly, "that will not work. The difference between my mother and you is this: You heard her story; she had no story to go by."

After a saint has used a ladder, it is thrown away, never to be used again.

•

Wife to husband whose face is buried in the newspaper: "Has it ever occurred to you that there might be more to life than what's going on in the world?"

Most people love humanity. It's the person next door they cannot stand.

•

Human beings react not to reality, but to ideas in their heads.

A group of tourists, stranded somewhere in the countryside, was given old rations to eat. Before eating the food, they tested it by throwing some of it to a dog, who seemed to enjoy it and suffered no aftereffects.

The following day they learned that the dog had died. Everyone was panic-stricken. Many began to vomit and complained of fever and dysentery. A doctor was called in to treat the victims for food poisoning.

The doctor began by asking what had happened to the body of the dog. Inquiries were made. A neighbor said casually, "Oh, it was thrown in a ditch because it got run over by a car."

•

The walls that imprison them are mental, not real.

A bear paced up and down the twenty feet that was the length of his cage.

When, after five years, the cage was removed, the bear continued to pace up and down those twenty feet as if the cage were there. It was. For him!

•

Instead of touching reality they respond to stereotypes....

At the final dinner of an international conference, an American delegate turned to the Chinese delegate sitting next to him, pointed to the soup, and asked, somewhat condescendingly, "Likee soupee?" The Chinese gentleman nodded eagerly.

A little later it was, "Likee fishee?" and "Likee meatee?" and "Likee fruitee?" — and always the response was an affable nod.

At the end of the dinner the chairman of the conference introduced the guest speaker of the evening — none other than the Chinese gentleman, who delivered a penetrating, witty discourse in impeccable English, much to the astonishment of his American neighbor.

When the speech was over, the speaker turned to his neighbor and, with a mischievous twinkle in his eye, asked, "Likee speechee?"

•

A man said to his parish priest, "My dog died yesterday, Father. Could you offer a Mass for the repose of his soul?"

The priest was outraged. "We don't offer Masses for animals here," he said sharply. "You might try the new denomination down the road. They'll probably pray for your dog."

"I really loved that little fellow," said the man, "and I'd like to give him a decent send-off. I don't know what it is customary to offer on such occasions, but do you think five hundred thousand dollars would do?"

"Now wait a minute," said the priest. "You never told me your dog was a Catholic!"

•

All that you give to others you are giving to yourself.

Once upon a time the members of the body were very annoyed with the stomach. They were resentful that they had to procure food and bring it to the stomach while the stomach itself did nothing but devour the fruit of their labor.

So they decided they would no longer bring the stomach food. The hands would not lift it to the mouth. The teeth would not chew it. The throat would not swallow it. That would force the stomach to do something.

But all they succeeded in doing was make the body weak to the point that they were threatened with death. So it was finally they who learned the lesson that in helping one another they were really working for their own welfare.

•

I get a great kick out of serving you — but I still insist that you be grateful.

A bejeweled dowager stepped out of a fashionable hotel in London where she had been dining and dancing all evening at a charity ball for the support of street urchins.

She was about to get into her Rolls Royce when a street urchin walked up to her and whined, "Spare me sixpence, ma'am, for charity. I haven't eaten for two days."

The duchess recoiled from the kid. "You ungrateful wretch!" she exclaimed. "Don't you realize I have been dancing for you all night?"

•

Once upon a time there was an inn called the Silver Star. The innkeeper was unable to make ends meet even though he did his very best to draw customers by making the inn comfortable, the service cordial, and the prices reasonable. So in despair he consulted a sage.

After listening to his tale of woe, the sage said, "It is very simple. You must change the name of your inn."

"Impossible!" said the innkeeper. "It has been the Silver Star for generations and is well known all over the country."

"No," said the sage firmly. "You must now call it the Five Bells and have a row of six bells hanging at the entrance."

"Six bells? But that's absurd. What good would that do?"

"Give it a try and see," said the sage with a smile.

Well, the innkeeper gave it a try. And this is what he saw. Every traveler who passed by the inn walked in to point out the mistake, each one believing that no one else had noticed it. Once inside, they were impressed by the cordiality of the service and stayed on to refresh themselves, thereby providing the innkeeper with the fortune that he had been seeking in vain for so long.

There are few things the ego delights in more than correcting other people's mistakes.

•

Every month the disciple faithfully sent his master an account of his spiritual progress.

In the first month he wrote, "I feel an expansion of consciousness and experience my oneness with the universe." The master glanced at the note and threw it away.

The following month this is what he had to say: "I have finally discovered that the divine is present in all things." The master seemed disappointed.

In his third letter the disciple enthusiastically explained, "The mystery of the One and the many has been revealed to my wondering gaze." The master yawned.

His next letter said, "No one is born, no one lives, and no one dies, for the self is not." The master threw his hands up in despair.

After that a month passed by, then two, then five; then a whole year. The master thought it was time to remind his disciple of his duty to keep him informed of his spiritual progress. The disciple wrote back, "Who cares?" When the master read those words, a look of satisfaction spread over his face. He said. "Thank God, at last he's got it!"

•

A great and foolish king complained that the rough ground hurt his feet, so he ordered the whole country to be carpeted with cowhide.

The court jester laughed when the king told him of his order. "What an absolutely crazy idea, Your Majesty," he cried. "Why all the needless expense? Just cut out two small pads to protect your feet!"

That is what the king did. And that is how the idea of shoes was born.

The enlightened know that to make the world a painless place, you need to change your heart — not the world.

•

The disciples asked the master to speak to them of death: "What will it be like?"

"It will be as if a veil is ripped apart and you will say in wonder, 'So it was You all along?' "

•

A merchant in Baghdad sent his servant on an errand to the bazaar, and the man came back white with fear and trembling. "Master," he said, "while I was in the marketplace, I walked into a stranger. When I looked him in the face, I found that it was Death. He made a threatening gesture at me and walked away. Now I am afraid. Please give me a horse so that I can ride at once to Samarra and put as great a distance as possible between Death and me."

The merchant — in his anxiety for the man — gave him his swiftest steed. The servant was on it and away in a trice. Later in the day the merchant himself went down to the bazaar and saw Death loitering there in the crowd. So he went up to him and said, "You made a threatening gesture at my poor servant this morning. What did it mean?"

"That was no threatening gesture, sir," said Death. "It was a start of surprise at seeing him here in Baghdad."

"Why would he not be in Baghdad? This is where the man lives."

"Well, I had been given to understand that he would join me in Samarra tonight, you see."

Most people are so afraid to die that, from their efforts to avoid death, they never live.

•

There was once a huge dragon in China who went from village to village killing cattle and dogs and chickens and children indiscriminately. So the villagers called upon a wizard to help them in their distress. The wizard said, "I cannot slay the dragon myself for, magician though I am, I am too afraid. But I shall find you the man who will."

With that he transformed himself into a dragon and took up a position on a bridge, so everyone who did not know it was the wizard was afraid to pass. One day, however, a traveler came up to the bridge, calmly climbed over the dragon, and walked on.

The wizard promptly took on human shape again and called

to the man. "Come back, my friend, I have been standing here for weeks waiting for you!"

The enlightened know that fear is in the way you look at things, not in the things themselves.

•

A shepherd was grazing his sheep when a passerby said, "That's a fine flock of sheep you have. Could I ask you something about them?"

"Of course," said the shepherd.

Said the man, "How much would you say your sheep walk each day?"

"Which ones, the white ones or the black ones?"

"The white ones."

"Well, the white ones walk about four miles a day."

"And the black ones?"

"The black ones too."

"And how much grass would you say they eat each day?"

"Which ones, the white or the black?"

"The white ones."

"Well, the white ones eat about four pounds of grass each day."

"And the black ones?"

"The black ones too."

"And how much wool would you say they give each year?"

"Which ones, the white or the black?"

"The white ones."

"Well, I'd say the white ones give some six pounds of wool each year at shearing time."

"And the black ones?"

"The black ones too."

The passerby was intrigued. "May I ask you why you have this strange habit of dividing your sheep into white and black each time you answer one of my questions?"

"Well," said the shepherd, "that's only natural. The white ones are mine, you see."

"Ah! And the black ones?"

"The black ones too," said the shepherd.

The human mind makes foolish divisions in what Love sees as One.

•

Plutarch tells the story of how Alexander the Great came upon Diogenes looking attentively at a heap of human bones.

"What are you looking for?" asked Alexander.

"Something that I cannot find," said the philosopher.

"And what is that?"

"The difference between your father's bones and those of his slaves."

The following are just as indistinguishable: Catholic bones from Protestant bones. Hindu bones from Muslim bones. Arab bones from Israeli bones. Russian bones from American bones.

The enlightened fail to see the difference even when the bones are clothed in flesh!

•

The human condition is perfectly depicted in the case of the poor drunk standing late at night outside the park, beating on the fence, and yelling. "Let me out!"

Only your illusions prevent you from seeing that you are — and always have been — free.

•

Mamiya became a well-known Zen master. But he had to learn Zen the hard way. While he was a disciple, his master asked him to explain the sound of one hand clapping.

Mamiya gave it all he had, skimping on food and sleep so that he could come up with the correct answer. But his master was never satisfied. He even said to him one day, "You're not working hard enough. You are far too comfort-loving, too attached to the good things of life, even too attached to finding the answer as quickly as possible. It would be better if you died."

The next time Mamiya came before the master, he did something dramatic. When asked to explain the sound of one hand clapping, he fell over and stayed still as if he were dead.

Said the master, "All right. So you're dead. But what about the sound of one hand clapping?"

Opening his eyes, Mamiya replied, "I haven't been able to solve that one yet."

At this the master shouted in fury, "Fool! Dead men don't speak. Get out!"

You may not be enlightened but you could at least be consistent!

•

Anand was Buddha's most devoted disciple. Years after Buddha's death a Great Council of the Enlightened was planned and one of the disciples went to tell Anand about it.

Now at that time Anand was still not enlightened himself, though he had worked at it strenuously for years. So he was not entitled to attend the council.

On the evening of the council meeting he was still not enlightened, so he determined to practice vigorously all night and not stop till he had attained his goal. But all he succeeded in doing was making himself exhausted. He had not made the slightest progress in spite of all his efforts.

So toward dawn he decided to give up and get some rest. In that state in which he had lost all greed, even for enlightenment, he rested his head on the pillow. And he suddenly became enlightened!

Said the river to the seeker, "Does one really have to fret about enlightenment? No matter which way I turn, I'm homeward bound."

7

Awareness

A de Mello Spirituality Conference in His Own Words

On Waking Up

Spirituality means waking up. Most people, even though they don't know it, are asleep. They're born asleep, they live asleep, they marry in their sleep, they breed children in their sleep, they die in their sleep without ever waking up. They never understand the loveliness and the beauty of this thing that we call human existence. You know, all mystics — Catholic, Christian, non-Christian, no matter what their theology, no matter what their religion — are unanimous on one thing: that all is well, all is well. Though everything is a mess, all is well. Strange paradox, to be sure. But, tragically, most people never get to see that all is well because they are asleep. They are having a nightmare....

Waking up is unpleasant, you know. You are nice and comfortable in bed. It's irritating to be woken up. That's the reason the wise guru will not attempt to wake people up. I hope I'm going to be wise here and make no attempt whatsoever to wake you up if you are asleep. It is really none of my business, even though I say to you at times, "Wake up!" My business is to do my thing, to dance my dance. If you profit from it, fine; if you don't, too bad! As the Arabs say, "The nature of rain is the same, but it makes thorns grow in the marshes and flowers in the gardens."

Self-Observation

The only way someone can be of help to you is in challenging your ideas. If you're ready to listen and if you're ready to be challenged, there's one thing that you can do, but *no one can help you*. What is this most important thing of all? It's called self-observation. No one can help you there. No one can give you a method. No one can show you a technique. The moment you pick up a technique, you're programmed again. But self-observation — watching yourself — is important. It is not the same as self-absorption. Self-absorption is self-preoccupation, where you're concerned about yourself, worried about yourself. I'm talking about self-*observation*. What's that? It means to watch everything in you and around you as far as possible and watch it as if it were happening to someone else. What does that last sentence mean? It means that you do not personalize what is happening to you. It means that you look at things as if you have no connection with them whatsoever.

The reason you suffer from your depression and your anxieties is that you identify with them. You say, "I'm depressed." But that is false. You are not depressed. If you want to be accurate, you might say, "I am experiencing a depression right now." But you can hardly say, "I am depressed." You are not your depression. That is but a strange kind of trick of the mind, a strange kind of illusion. You have deluded yourself into thinking — though you are not aware of it — that you *are* your depression, that you *are* your anxiety, that you *are* your joy or the thrills that you have. "I am delight!" You certainly are not delighted. Delight may be *in* you right now, but wait around, it will change; it won't last: it never lasts; it keeps changing: it's always changing. Clouds come and go: Some of them are black and some white, some of them are large, others small. If we want to follow the analogy, you would be the sky, observing the clouds. You are a passive, detached observer. That's shocking, particularly to someone in the Western culture. You're not interfering. Don't interfere. Don't "fix" anything. Watch! Observe!

The trouble with people is that they're busy fixing things they don't even understand. We're always fixing things, aren't we? It never strikes us that things don't need to be fixed. They really don't. This is a great illumination. They need to be understood. If you understood them, they'd change.

Awareness without Evaluating Everything

Do you want to change the world? How about beginning with yourself? How about being transformed yourself first? But how do you achieve that? Through observation. Through understanding. With no interference or judgment on your part. Because what you judge you cannot understand.

There's nothing so delightful as being aware. Would you rather live in darkness? Would you rather act and not be aware of your actions, talk and not be aware of your words? Would you rather listen to people and not be aware of what you're hearing, or see things and not be aware of what you're looking at? The great Socrates said, "The unaware life is not worth living." That's a self-evident truth. Most people don't live aware lives. They live mechanical lives, mechanical thoughts — generally somebody else's — mechanical emotions, mechanical actions, mechanical reactions. Do you want to see how mechanical you really are? "My, that's a lovely shirt you're wearing." You feel good hearing that. For a shirt, for heaven's sake! You feel proud of yourself when you hear that. People come over to my center in India and they say, "What a lovely place, these lovely trees" (for which I'm not responsible at all), "this lovely climate." And already I'm feeling good, until I catch myself feeling good, and I say, "Hey, can you imagine anything as stupid as that?" I'm not responsible for those trees; I wasn't responsible for choosing the location. I didn't order the weather; it just happened. But "me" got in there, so I'm feeling good. I'm feeling good about "my" culture and "my" nation. How stupid can you get? I mean that. I'm told my great Indian culture has produced all these mystics. I didn't produce them. I'm not responsible for them. Or they tell me, "That country of yours and its poverty — it's disgusting." I feel ashamed. But I didn't create it. What's going on? Did you ever stop to think? People tell you, "I think you're very charming," so I feel wonderful. I get a positive stroke (that's why they call it I'm O.K., you're O.K.). I'm going to write a book someday and the title will be *I'm an Ass, You're an Ass.* That's the most liberating, wonderful thing in the world, when you openly admit you're an ass. It's wonderful. When people tell me, "You're wrong." I say, "What can you expect of an ass?"

Disarmed, everybody has to be disarmed. In the final liberation, I'm an ass, you're an ass. Normally the way it goes, I press a button and you're up; I press another button and you're down. And you like that. How many people do you know who are unaffected by praise or blame? That isn't human, we say. Human means that you have to be a little monkey, so everybody can twist your tail, and you do whatever you *ought* to be doing. But is that human? If you find me charming, it means that right now you're in a good mood, nothing more.

Awareness and Contact with Reality

To watch everything inside of you and outside, and when there is something happening to you, to see it as if it were happening to someone else, with no comment, no judgment, no attitude, no interference, no attempt to change, only to understand. As you do this, you'll begin to realize that increasingly you are disidentifying from "me." St. Teresa of Avila says that toward the end of her life God gave her an extraordinary grace. She doesn't use this modern expression, of course, but what it really boils down to is disidentifying from herself. If someone else has cancer and I don't know the person, I'm not all that affected. If I had love and sensitivity, maybe I'd help, but I'm not emotionally affected. If *you* have an examination to take, I'm not all that affected. I can be quite philosophical about it and say, "Well, the more you worry about it, the worse it'll get. Why not just take a good break instead of studying?" But when it's my turn to have an examination, well, that's something else, isn't it? The reason is that I've identified with "me" — with my family, my country, my possessions, my body, me. How would it be if God gave me grace not to call these things mine? I'd be detached; I'd be disidentified. That's what it means to lose the self, to deny the self, to die to self.

Four Steps to Wisdom

The first thing you need to do is get in touch with negative feelings that you're not even aware of. Lots of people have negative feelings they're not aware of. Lots of people are depressed and they're not aware they are depressed. It's only when they make contact with joy that they understand how depressed they were. You can't deal with a cancer that you haven't detected. You can't get rid of boll weevils on your farm if you're not aware of their existence. The first thing you need is awareness of your negative feelings. What negative feelings? Gloominess, for instance. You're feeling gloomy and moody. You feel self-hatred or guilt. You feel that life is pointless, that it makes no sense; you've got hurt feelings, you're feeling nervous and tense. Get in touch with those feelings first.

The second step (this is a four-step program) is to understand that the feeling is in you, not in reality. That's such a self-evident thing, but do you think people know it? They don't, believe me. They've got Ph.D.s and are presidents of universities, but they haven't understood this. They didn't teach me how to live at school. They taught me everything else. As one man said, "I got a pretty good education. It took me years to get over it." That's what spirituality is all about, you know: unlearning. Unlearning all the rubbish they taught you.

The third step: Never identify with that feeling. It has nothing to do with the "I." Don't define your essential self in terms of that feeling. Don't say, "I am depressed." If you want to say, "It is depressed," that's all right. If you want to say depression is there, that's fine; if you want to say gloominess is there, that's fine. But not: I am gloom. You're defining yourself in terms of the feeling. That's your illusion; that's your mistake. There is a depression there right now, there are hurt feelings there right now, but let it be, leave it alone. It will pass. Everything passes, everything. Your depression and your thrills have nothing to do with happiness. Those are the swings of the pendulum. If you seek kicks or thrills, get ready for depression. Do you want your drug? Get ready for the hangover. One end of the pendulum swings to the other.

The fourth step: How do you change things? How do you change yourselves? There are many things you must understand here, or rather, just one thing that can be expressed in many ways. Imagine a patient who goes to a doctor and tells him what he is suffering from. The doctor says, "Very well, I've understood your symptoms. Do you know what I will do? I will prescribe a medicine for your neighbor!" The patient replies, "Thank you very much, Doctor, that makes me feel much better." Isn't that absurd? But that's what we all do. The person who is asleep always thinks he'll feel better if somebody else changes. You're suffering because you are asleep, but you're thinking, "How wonderful life would be if somebody else would change; how wonderful life would be if my neighbor changed, my wife changed, my boss changed."

We always want someone else to change so that we will feel good. But has it ever struck you that even if your wife changes or your husband changes, what does that do to you? You're just as vulnerable as before; you're just as idiotic as before; you're just as asleep as before. You are the one who needs to change, who needs to take medicine. You keep insisting, "I feel good because the world is right." *Wrong!* The world is right because I feel good. That's what all the mystics are saying.

Arriving at Silence

The fanaticism of one sincere believer who thinks he knows causes more evil than the united efforts of two hundred rogues. It's terrifying to see what sincere believers will do because they think they know. Wouldn't it be wonderful if we had a world where everybody said, "We don't know"? One big barrier dropped. Wouldn't that be marvelous?

A man born blind comes to me and asks, "What is this thing called green?" How does one describe the color green to someone who was born blind? One uses analogies. So I say, "The color green is something like soft music." "Oh," he says, "like soft music." "Yes," I say, "soothing and soft music." So a second blind man comes to me and asks, "What is the color green?" I tell him it's something like soft satin, very soft and soothing to the touch. So the next day I notice that the two blind men are bashing each other over the head with bottles. One is saying, "It's soft like music"; the other is saying, "It's soft like satin." And on it goes. Neither of them knows what they're talking about, because if they did, they'd shut up. It's as bad as that. It's even worse, because one day, say, you give sight to this blind man, and he's sitting there in the garden and he's looking all around him, and you say to him, "Well, now you know what the color green is." And he answers, "That's true. I heard some of it this morning!"

The fact is that you're surrounded by God and you don't see God, because you "know" about God. The final barrier to the vision of God is your God concept. You miss God because you think you know. That's the terrible thing about religion. That's what the gospels were saying, that religious people "knew," so they got rid of Jesus. The highest knowledge of God is to know God as unknowable. There is far too much God talk; the world is sick of it. There is too little awareness, too little love, too little happiness, but let's not use those words either. There's too little dropping of illusions, dropping of errors, dropping of attachments and cruelty, too little awareness. That's what the world is suffering from, not from a lack of religion. Religion is supposed to be about a lack of awareness, of waking up. Look what we've degenerated into. Come to my country and see them killing one another over religion. You'll find it everywhere. "The one who knows, does not say; the one who says, does not know." All revelations, however divine, are never any more than a finger pointing to the moon. As we say in the East, "When the sage points to the moon, all the idiot sees is the finger."

At a Loss for Words

"Quia de deo scire non possumus quid sit, sed quid non sit, non possumus considerare de deo, quomodo sit sed quomodo non sit." This is St. Thomas Aquinas's introduction to his whole *Summa Theologica:* "Since we cannot know what God is, but only what God is not, we cannot consider how God is but only how He is not." In Thomas's commentary on Boethius's *De Sancta Trinitate,* he says that the loftiest degree of the knowledge of God is to know God as the unknown, *tamquam ignotum.* And in his *Quaestio Disputata de Potencia Dei,* Thomas says, "This is what is ultimate in the human knowledge of God — to know that we do not know God." This gentleman was considered the prince of theologians. He was a mystic and is a canonized saint today. We're standing on pretty good ground.

In India, we have a Sanskrit saying for this kind of thing: *neti, neti.* It means: "not that, not that." Thomas's own method was referred to as the *via negativa,* the negative way.

This is what is ultimate in our human knowledge of God, to know that we do not know. Our great tragedy is that we know too much. We *think* we know, that is our tragedy; so we never discover. In fact, Thomas Aquinas (he's not only a theologian but also a great philosopher) says repeatedly, "All the efforts of the human mind cannot exhaust the essence of a single fly."

Filtered Reality

I want to say one more thing about our perception of reality. Let me put it in the form of an analogy. The president of the United States has to get feedback from the citizens. The pope in Rome has to get feedback from the whole church. There are literally millions of items that could be fed to them, but they could hardly take all of them in, much less digest them. So they have people whom they trust to make abstracts, summarize things, monitor, filter; in the end, some of it gets to their desk. Now, this is what's happening to us. From every pore or living cell of our bodies and from all our senses we are getting feedback from reality. But we are filtering things out constantly. Who's doing the filtering? Our conditioning? Our culture? Our programming? The way we were taught to see things and to experience them? Even our language can be a filter. There is so much filtering going on that sometimes you won't see things that are there. You only have to look at paranoid people who are always feeling threatened by something that isn't there, who are constantly interpreting reality in terms of certain experiences of the past or certain conditioning that they have had.

But there's another demon, too, who's doing the filtering. It's called attachment, desire, craving. The root of sorrow is craving. Craving distorts and destroys perception. Fears and desires haunt us. Samuel Johnson said, "The knowledge that he is to swing from a scaffold within a week wonderfully concentrates a man's mind." You blot out everything else and concentrate only on the fear, or desire, or craving. In many ways we were drugged when we were young. We were brought up to need people. For what? For acceptance, approval, appreciation, applause — for what they called success. Those are words that do not correspond to reality. They are conventions, things that are invented, but we don't realize that they don't correspond to reality. What is success? It is what one group decided is a good thing. Another group will decide the same thing is bad. What is good in Washington might be considered bad in a Carthusian monastery. Success in a political circle might be considered failure in some other circles. These are conventions. But we treat them like realities, don't we? When we were young, we were programmed to unhappiness. They taught us that in order to be happy you need money, success, a beautiful or handsome partner in life, a good job, friendship, spirituality, God — you name it. Unless you get these things, you're not going to be happy, we were told. Now, that is what I call an attachment. An attachment is a belief that without something you are not going to be happy. Once you get convinced of that — and it gets into our subconscious, it gets stamped into the roots of our being — you are finished.

Insight and Understanding

But what does self-change entail? I've said it in so many words, over and over, but now I'm going to break it down into little segments. First, insight. Not effort, not cultivating habits, not having an idea. Ideals do a lot of damage. The whole time you're focusing on what should be instead of focusing on what is. And so you're imposing what should be on a present reality, never having understood what present reality is. Let me give you an example of insight from my own experience in counseling. A priest comes to me and says he's lazy; he wants to be more industrious, more active, but he is lazy. I ask him what "lazy" means. In the old days I would have said to him, "Let's see, why don't you make a list of things you want to do every day, and then every night you check them off, and it will give you a good feeling; build up habit that way." Or I might say to him, "Who is your ideal, your patron saint?" And if he says St. Francis Xavier, I would tell him, "See how much Xavier worked. You must meditate on him and that will get you moving." That's one way of going about it, but, I'm sorry to say, it's superficial. Making him use his willpower, effort, doesn't last very long. His behavior may change, but he does not. So I now move in the other direction. I say to him, "Lazy, what's that? There are a million types of laziness. Let's hear what your type of laziness is. Describe what *you* mean by lazy." He says, "Well, I never get anything done. I don't feel like doing anything." I ask, "You mean right from the moment you get up in the morning?" "Yes," he answers. "I wake up in the morning and there's nothing worth getting up for." "You're depressed, then?" I ask. "You could call it that," he says. "I have sort of withdrawn." "Have you always been like this?" I ask. "Well, not always. When I was younger, I was more active. When I was in the seminary, I was full of life." "So when did this begin?" "Oh, about three or four years ago." I ask him if anything happened then. He thinks a while. I say, "If you have to think so much, nothing very special could have happened four years ago. How about the year before that?" He says, "Well, I was ordained that year." "Anything happen in your ordination year?" I ask. "There was one little thing, the final examination in theology; I failed it. It was a bit of a disappointment, but I've gotten over it. The bishop was planning to send me to Rome, to eventually teach in the seminary. I rather liked the idea, but since I failed the examination, he changed his mind and sent me to this parish. Actually, there was some injustice because...." Now he's getting worked up; there's anger there that he hasn't gotten over. He's got to work through that disappointment. It's useless to preach him a sermon. It's useless to give him an idea. We've got to get him to face his anger and disappointment and to get some insight into all of that. When he's able to work through that, he's back into life again. If I gave him an exhortation and told him how hard his married brothers and sisters work, that would merely make him feel guilty. He doesn't have the self-insight which is going to heal him. So that's the first thing.

There's another great task, understanding. Did you really think this was going to make you happy? You just assumed it was going to make you happy. Why did you want to teach in the seminary? Because you wanted to be happy. You thought that being a professor, having a certain status and prestige, would make you happy. Would it? Understanding is called for there.

Not Pushing It

Meditating on and imitating externally the behavior of Jesus is no help. It's not a question of imitating Christ; it's a question of becoming what Jesus was. It's a question of becoming Christ, becoming aware, understanding what's going on within you. All the other methods we use for self-change could be compared to pushing a car. Let's suppose you have to travel to a distant city. The car breaks down along the way. Well, too bad; the car's broken down. So we roll up our sleeves and begin to push the car. And we push and push and push and push, till we get to the distant city. "Well," we say, "We made it." And then we push the car all the way to another city! You say, "We got there, didn't we?" But do you call this life? You know what you need? You need an expert, you need a mechanic to lift the hood and change the spark plug. Turn the ignition key and the car moves. You need the expert — you need understanding, insight, awareness. You don't need pushing. You don't need effort. That's why people are so tired, so weary. You and I were trained to be dissatisfied with ourselves. That's where the evil comes from psychologically. We're always dissatisfied, we're always discontented, we're always pushing. Go on, put out more effort, more and more effort. But there's always that conflict inside; there's very little understanding.

Getting Real

One red-letter day in my life occurred in India. It was a great day, really, the day after I was ordained. I sat in a confessional. We had a very saintly Jesuit priest in our parish, a Spaniard, whom I had known even before I went to the Jesuit novitiate. The day before I left for the novitiate, I thought I'd better make a clean breast of everything so that when I got to the noviciate I'd be nice and clean and wouldn't have to tell the novice master anything. This old Spanish priest would have crowds of people lined up at his confessional; he had a violet-colored handkerchief which he covered his eyes with, and he'd mumble something and give you a penance and send you away. He'd only met me a couple of times, but he'd call me Antonie. So I stood in line, and when my turn came, I tried changing my voice as I made my confession. He listened to me patiently, gave me my penance, absolved me, and then said, "Antonie, when are you going to the novitiate?"

Well, anyway, I went to this parish the day after my ordination. And the old priest says to me, "Do you want to hear confessions?" I said, "All right." He said, "Go and sit in my confessional." I thought, "My, I'm a holy man. I'm going to sit in his confessional." I heard confessions for three hours. It was Palm Sunday and we had the Easter crowd coming in. I came out depressed, not from what I had heard, because I had been led to expect that, and, having some inkling of what was going on in my own heart, I was shocked by nothing. You know what depressed me? The realization that I was giving them these little pious platitudes: "Now pray to the Blessed Mother, she loves you," and "Remember that God is on your side." Were these pious platitudes any cure for cancer? And this is a cancer I'm dealing with, the lack of awareness and reality. So I swore a mighty oath to myself that day: "I'll learn, I'll learn, so it will not be said of me when it is all over, 'Father, what you said to me was absolutely true but totally useless.'"

Awareness, insight. When you become an expert (and you'll soon become an expert) you don't need to take a course in psychology. As you begin to observe yourself, to watch yourself, to pick up those negative feelings, you'll find your own way of explaining it. And you'll notice the change. But then you'll have to deal with the big villain, and that villain is self-condemnation, self-hatred, self-dissatisfaction.

Assorted Images

Let's talk more about effortlessness in change. I thought of a nice image for that, a sailboat. When a sailboat has a mighty wind in its sail, it glides along so effortlessly that the boatman has nothing to do but steer. He makes no effort; he doesn't push the boat. That's an image of what happens when change comes about through awareness, through understanding.

I was going through some of my notes, and I found some quotations that go well with what I've been saying. Listen to this one: "There is nothing so cruel as nature. In the whole universe there is no escape from it, and yet it is not nature that does the injury, but the person's own heart." Does that make sense? It isn't nature that does the injury, but the person's own heart. There's the story of Paddy, who fell off the scaffolding and got a good bump. They asked, "Did the fall hurt you, Paddy?" And he said, "No, it was the stop that hurt, not the fall." When you cut water, the water doesn't get hurt; when you cut something solid, it breaks. You've got solid attitudes inside you; you've got solid illusions inside you; that's what bumps against nature, that's where you get hurt, that's where the pain comes from.

Here's a lovely one: It's from an Oriental sage, though I don't remember which one. As with the Bible the author doesn't matter. What is said is what matters. "If the eye is unobstructed, it results in sight; if the ear is unobstructed, the result is hearing; if the nose is unobstructed, the result is a sense of smell; if the mouth is unobstructed, the result is a sense of taste; if the mind is unobstructed, the result is wisdom."

Wisdom occurs when you drop barriers you have erected through your concepts and conditioning. Wisdom is not something acquired; wisdom is not experience; wisdom is not applying yesterday's illusions to today's problems. As somebody said to me while I was studying for my degree in psychology in Chicago years ago, "Frequently, in the life of a priest, fifty years' experience is one year's experience repeated fifty times." You get the same solutions to fall back on: This is the way to deal with the alcoholic; this is the way to deal with priests; this is the way to deal with sisters; this is the way to deal with a divorcée. But that isn't wisdom. Wisdom is to be sensitive to *this* situation, to *this* person, uninfluenced by any carryover from the past, without residue from the experience of the past. This is quite unlike what most people are accustomed to thinking. I would add another sentence to the ones I've read: "If the heart is unobstructed, the result is love." I've been talking a great deal about love these days even though I told you there's nothing that can be said, really, about love. We can only speak of non-love. We can only speak of addictions. But of love itself nothing may be said explicitly.

Losing Control

If you wish to understand control, think of a little child that is given a taste for drugs. As the drugs penetrate the body of the child, it becomes addicted; its whole being cries out for the drug. To be without the drug is so unbearable a torment that it seems preferable to die. Think of that image — the body has gotten addicted to the drug. Now this is exactly what your society did to you when you were born. You were not allowed to enjoy the solid, nutritious food of life — namely, work, play, fun, laughter, the company of people, the pleasures of the senses and the mind. You were given a taste for the drug called approval, appreciation, attention.

I'm going to quote a great man here, a man named A. S. Neill. He is the author of *Summerhill.* Neill says that the sign of a sick child is that he is always hovering around his parents; he is interested in *persons.* The healthy child has no interest in persons, he is interested in *things.* When a child is sure of his mother's love, he forgets his mother; he goes out to explore the world; he is curious. He looks for a frog to put in his mouth —

that kind of thing. When a child is hovering around his mother, it's a bad sign; he's insecure. Maybe his mother has been trying to suck love *out* of him, not giving him all the freedom and assurance he wants. His mother has always been threatening in many subtle ways to abandon him.

So we were given a taste of various drug addictions: approval, attention, success, making it to the top, prestige, getting your name in the paper, power, being the boss. We were given a taste like being the captain of the team, leading the band, etc. Having a taste for these drugs, we became addicted and began to dread losing them. Recall the lack of control you felt, the terror at the prospect of failure or of making mistakes, at the prospect of criticism by others. So you became cravenly dependent on others and you lost your freedom. Others now have the power to make you happy or miserable. You crave your drugs, but as much as you hate the suffering that this involves, you find yourself completely helpless. There is never a minute when, consciously or unconsciously, you are not aware of or attuned to the reactions of others, marching to the beat of their drums. A nice definition of an awakened person: a person who no longer marches to the drums of society, a person who dances to the tune of the music that springs up from within. When you are ignored or disapproved of, you experience a loneliness so unbearable that you crawl back to people and beg for the comforting drug called support and encouragement, reassurance. To live with people in this state involves a never-ending tension. "Hell is other people," said Sartre. How true. When you are in this state of dependency, you always have to be on your best behavior; you can never let your hair down; you have to live up to expectations. To be with people is to live in tension. To be without them brings the agony of loneliness, because you miss them. You have lost your capacity to see them exactly as they are and to respond to them accurately, because your perception of them is clouded by the need to get your drugs. You see them insofar as they are a support for getting your drug or a threat to have your drug removed. You're always looking at people, consciously or unconsciously, through these eyes. Will I get what I want from them, will I not get what I want from them? And if they can neither support nor threaten my drug, I'm not interested in them. That's a horrible thing to say, but I wonder if there's anyone here of whom this cannot be said.

The Land of Love

If we really dropped illusions for what they can give us or deprive us of, we would be alert. The consequence of not doing this is terrifying and unescapable. We lose our capacity to love. If you wish to love, you must learn to see again. And if you wish to see, you must learn to give up your drug. It's as simple as that. Give up your dependency. Tear away the tentacles of society that have enveloped and suffocated your being. You must drop them. Externally, everything will go on as before, but though you will continue to be *in* the world, you will no longer be *of* it. In your heart, you will now be free at last, if utterly alone. Your dependence on your drug will die. You don't have to go to the desert; you're right in the middle of people; you're enjoying them immensely. But they no longer have the power to make you happy or miserable. That's what aloneness means. In this solitude your dependence dies. The capacity to love is born. One no longer sees others as means of satisfying one's addiction. Only someone who has attempted this knows the terrors of the process. It's like inviting yourself to die. It's like asking the poor drug addict to give up the only happiness he has ever known. How to replace it with the taste of bread and fruit and the clean taste of the morning air, the sweetness of the water of the mountain stream? While he is struggling with his withdrawal symptoms and the emptiness he experiences within himself now that his drug is gone, nothing can fill the emptiness except his drug. Can you imagine a life in which you refuse to enjoy or take pleasure in a single word of appreciation or to rest your head on anyone's shoulder for support? Think of a life in which you depend on no one emotionally, so that no one has the power to make you happy or miserable anymore. You refuse to *need* any particular person or to be special to anyone or to call anyone your own. The birds of the air have their nests and the foxes their holes, but you will have nowhere to rest your head in your journey through life. If you ever get to this state, you will at last know what it means to see with a vision that is clear and unclouded by fear or desire. Every word there is measured. *To see at last with a vision that is clear and unclouded by fear or desire.* You will know what it means to love. But to come to the land of love, you must pass through the pains of death, for to love persons means to die to the need for persons and to be utterly alone.

Let me end this with a lovely story. There was a man who invented the art of making fire. He took his tools and went to a tribe in the north, where it was very cold, bitterly cold. He taught the people there to make fire. The people were very interested. He showed them the uses to which they could put fire — they could cook, could keep themselves warm, etc. They were so grateful that they had learned the art of making fire. But before they could express their gratitude to the man, he disappeared. He wasn't concerned with getting their recognition or gratitude; he was concerned about their well-being. He went to another tribe, where he again began to show them the value of his invention. People were interested there, too, a bit too interested for the peace of mind of their priests, who began to notice that this man was drawing crowds and they were losing their popularity. So they decided to do away with him. They poisoned him, crucified him, put it any way you like. But they were afraid now that the people might turn against them, so they were very wise, even wily. Do you know what they did? They had a portrait of the man made and mounted it on the main altar of the temple. The instruments for making fire were placed in front of the portrait, and the people were taught to revere the portrait and to pay reverence to the instruments of fire, which they dutifully did for centuries. The veneration and the worship went on, but there was no fire.

Where's the fire? Where's the love? Where's the drug uprooted from your system? Where's the freedom? This is what spirituality is all about. Tragically, we tend to lose sight of this, don't we? This is what Jesus Christ is all about. But we overemphasized the "Lord, Lord," didn't we? Where's the fire? And if worship isn't leading to the fire, if adoration isn't leading to love, if the liturgy isn't leading to a clearer perception of reality, if God isn't leading to life, of what use is religion except to create more division, more fanaticism, more antagonism? It is not from lack of religion in the ordinary sense of the word that the world is suffering, it is from lack of love, lack of awareness. I have run into individuals, here and there, who suddenly stumble upon this truth: The root of evil is within you. As you begin to understand this, you stop making demands on yourself, you stop having expectations of yourself, you stop pushing yourself and you understand. Nourish yourself on wholesome food, good wholesome food. I'm not talking about actual food, I'm talking about sunset, about nature, about a good movie, about a good book, about enjoyable work, about good company, and hopefully you will break your addictions to those other feelings.

What kind of feeling comes upon you when you're in touch with nature, or when you're absorbed in work that you love? Or when you're really conversing with someone whose company you enjoy in openness and intimacy without clinging? What kind of feelings do you have? Compare those feelings with the feelings you have when you win an argument, or when you win a race, or when you become popular, or when everybody's applauding you. The latter feelings I call worldly feelings; the former feelings I call soul feelings. Lots of people gain the world and lose their soul. Lots of people live empty, soulless lives because they're feeding themselves on popularity, appreciation, and praise, on "I'm O.K., you're O.K.," look at me, attend to me, support me, value me, on being the boss, on having power, on winning the race. Do you feed yourself on that? If you do, you're dead. You've lost your soul. Feed yourself on other, more nourishing material. Then you'll see the transformation. I've given you a whole program for life, haven't I?

8

The Way to Love

Profit and Loss

*For what will it profit a man, if he gains the whole world
and forfeits his life?* — MATTHEW 16:26

Recall the kind of feeling you have when someone praises you,
when you are approved, accepted, applauded. And contrast that
with the kind of feeling that arises within you when you look at
the sunset or the sunrise or Nature in general, or when you read
a book or watch a movie that you thoroughly enjoy. Get the
taste of this feeling and contrast it with the first, namely, the one
that was generated within you when you were praised. Understand that the first type of feeling comes from self-glorification,
self-promotion. It is a worldly feeling. The second comes from
self-fulfillment, a soul feeling.

Here is another contrast: Recall the kind of feeling you have
when you succeed, when you have made it, when you get to the
top, when you win a game or a bet or an argument. And contrast it with the kind of feeling you get when you really enjoy
the job you are doing, you are absorbed in, the action that you
are currently engaged in. And once again notice the qualitative
difference between the worldly feeling and the soul feeling.

Yet another contrast: Remember what you felt like when you
had power, you were the boss, people looked up to you, took

126

orders from you; or when you were popular. And contrast that worldly feeling with the feeling of intimacy, companionship — the times you thoroughly enjoyed yourself in the company of a friend or with a group in which there was fun and laughter.

Having done this, attempt to understand the true nature of worldly feelings, namely, the feelings of self-promotion, self-glorification. They are not natural. They were invented by your society and your culture to make you productive and to make you controllable. These feelings do not produce the nourishment and happiness that are produced when one contemplates Nature or enjoys the company of one's friends or one's work. They were meant to produce thrills, excitement — and emptiness.

Heaven at Hand

> *Repent, for the kingdom of heaven is at hand.*
> — MATTHEW 4:17

Imagine you have a radio that no matter how you turn the knob picks up only one station. You have no control over the volume. At times the sound is barely audible, at others, it is so loud that it almost shatters your eardrums. Moreover, it is impossible to turn it off; at times it will be slow; it will suddenly begin to blare away when you want to rest and sleep. Who would put up with this kind of performance in a radio? And yet when your heart behaves in this kind of crazy fashion you not only put up with it but even call it normal and human.

Think of the numerous times you were tossed about by your emotions, that you have suffered the pangs of anger, depression, anxiety, when in every instance it was because your heart became set on getting something that you did not have, or on holding on to something that you had, or on avoiding something that you did not want. You were in love and you felt rejected or jealous; suddenly all your mind and heart became focused on this one thing, and the banquet of life turned to ashes in your mouth. You were bent on winning an election, and in the din of battle it was impossible to hear the songs of birds: Your ambition drowned out every other sound. You were faced with the possibility of a serious illness or the loss of a loved one and you found it impossible to concentrate on anything.

To put it briefly, the moment you pick up an attachment, the functioning of this lovely apparatus called the human heart is destroyed. If you want to repair your radio, you must study radio mechanics. If you want to reform your heart, you must give serious, prolonged thought to four liberating truths. But first choose some attachment that troubles you, something that you are clinging to, or something that you dread, or something you are craving for, and keep this attachment in mind as you listen to these truths.

The first truth: You must choose between your attachment and happiness. You cannot have both. The moment you pick up an attachment, your heart is thrown out of kilter and your ability to lead a joyful, carefree, serene life is destroyed. See how true this is when applied to the attachment that you have chosen.

The second truth: Where did your attachment come from? You were not born with it. It sprang from a lie that your society and your culture have told you, or a lie that you have told yourself, namely, that without this or the other, without this person or the other, you can't be happy. Just open your eyes and see how false this is. There are hundreds of persons who are perfectly happy without this thing or person or situation that you crave for and that you have convinced yourself you cannot live without. So make your choice: Do you want your attachment, or your freedom and happiness?

The third truth: If you wish to be fully alive you must develop a sense of perspective. Life is infinitely greater than this trifle your heart is attached to and which you have given the power to so upset you. Trifle, yes, because if you live long enough a day will easily come when it will cease to matter. It will not even be remembered — your own experience will confirm this. Just as today you barely remember, are no longer the least bit affected by those tremendous trifles that so disturbed you in the past.

And so the fourth truth brings you to the unavoidable conclusion that no thing or person outside of you has the power to make you happy or unhappy. Whether you are aware of it or not it is you and only you who decide to be happy or unhappy, whether you will cling to your attachment or not in any given situation.

What Must I Do?

> "*Teacher, what good deed must I do, to have eternal life?*"
> — MATTHEW 19:16

Think of yourself in a concert hall listening to the strains of the sweetest music when you suddenly remember that you forgot to lock your car. You are anxious about the car, you cannot walk out of the hall, and you cannot enjoy the music. There you have a perfect image of life as it is lived by most human beings.

For life to those who have the ears to hear is a symphony; but very, very rare indeed is the human being who hears the music. Why? Because we are busy listening to the noises that our conditioning and our programming have put into our heads. That and something else — our attachments. An attachment is a major killer of life. To really hear the symphony you must be sensitively attuned to every instrument in the orchestra. When you take pleasure only in the drum, you cease to hear the symphony because the sound of the drum has blotted out the other instruments. You may have your preferences for drum or violin or piano; no harm in these, for a preference does not damage your capacity to hear and enjoy the other instruments. But the moment your preference turns into an attachment, it hardens you to the other sounds, you suddenly undervalue them. And it blinds you to its particular instrument, for you give it a value out of all proportion to its merit.

Now look at a person or a thing you have an attachment for: someone or something to whom you have handed over the power to make you happy or unhappy. Observe how, because of your concentration on getting this person or thing and holding on to it and enjoying it exclusively to the exclusion of other things and persons, and how, because of your obsession with this person or thing, you have less sensitivity to the rest of the world. You have become hardened. And have the courage to see how prejudiced and blind you have become in the presence of this object of your attachment.

When you see this, you will feel a yearning to rid yourself of every attachment. The problem is, how? Renunciation and avoidance are no help, for to blot out the sound of the drum once again makes you as hard and insensitive as to concentrate solely on the drum. What you need is not renunciation but understanding, awareness. If your attachments have caused you suffering and sorrow, that's a help to understanding. If you have at least once in your life had the sweet taste of freedom and the delight in life that detachment brings, that too is a help. It also helps to consciously notice the sound of the other instruments in the orchestra. But there is no substitute for the awareness that shows you the loss you suffer when you overvalue the drum and when you turn a deaf ear to the rest of the orchestra.

Show No Partiality

"Teacher," they said, *"we know that you speak and teach rightly, and show no partiality."*   — LUKE 20:21

Look at your life and see how you have filled its emptiness with people. As a result they have a stranglehold on you. See how they control your behavior by their approval and disapproval. They hold the power to ease your loneliness with their company, to send your spirits soaring with their praise, to bring you down to the depths with their criticism and rejection. Take a look at yourself spending almost every waking minute of your day placating and pleasing people, whether they are living or dead. You live by their norms, conform to their standards, seek their company, desire their love, dread their ridicule, long for their applause, meekly submit to the guilt they lay upon you; you are terrified to go against the fashion in the way you dress or speak or act or even think.

And observe how even when you control them you depend on them and are enslaved by them.

People have become so much a part of your being that you cannot even imagine living a life that is unaffected or uncontrolled by them. As a matter of fact, they have convinced you that if you ever broke free of them, you would become an island — solitary, bleak, unloving. But the exact opposite is true. How can you love someone whom you are a slave to? How can you love someone whom you cannot live without? You can only desire, need, depend, fear, and be controlled. Love is to be found only in fearlessness and freedom. How do you achieve this freedom? By means of a two-pronged attack on your dependency and slavery. First, awareness. It is next to impossible to be dependent, to be a slave, when one constantly observes the folly of one's dependence. But awareness may not be enough for a person whose addiction is people. You must cultivate activities that you love. You must discover work that you do, not for its utility, but for itself. Think of something that you love to do for itself, whether it succeeds or not, whether you are praised for it or not, whether you are loved and rewarded for it or not, whether people know about it and are grateful to you for it or not. How many activities can you count in your life that you engage in simply because they delight you and grip your soul? Find them out, cultivate them, for they are your passport to freedom and to love.

Be Awake

> *Blessed are those servants whom the master finds awake when He comes.* — LUKE 12:37

Everywhere in the world people are in search of love, for everyone is convinced that love alone can save the world, love alone can make life meaningful and worth living. But how very few understand what love really is, and how it arises in the human heart. It is so frequently equated with good feelings toward others, with benevolence or nonviolence or service. But these things in themselves are not love. Love springs from awareness. It is only inasmuch as you see persons as they really are here and now and not as they are in your memory or your desire or in your imagination or projection that you can truly love them; otherwise it is not the people that you love but the idea that you have formed of them, or persons as the object of your desire, not as they are in themselves.

Therefore the first act of love is to see this person or this object, this reality as it truly is. And this involves the enormous discipline of dropping your desires, your prejudices, your memories, your projections, your selective way of looking, a discipline so great that most people would rather plunge headlong into good actions and service than submit to the burning fire of this asceticism. When you set out to serve someone whom you have not taken the trouble to see, are you meeting that person's need or your own? So the first ingredient of love is to really see the other.

The second ingredient is equally important: to see yourself, to ruthlessly flash the light of awareness on your motives, your emotions, your needs, your dishonesty, your self-seeking, your tendency to control and manipulate. This means calling things by their names, no matter how painful the discovery and the consequences. If you achieve this kind of awareness of the other and yourself, you will know what love is. For you will have attained a mind and a heart that are alert, vigilant, clear, sensitive, a clarity of perception, a sensitivity that will draw out of you an accurate, appropriate response to every situation at every moment. Sometimes you will be irresistibly impelled into action; at others you will be held back and restrained. You will sometimes be made to ignore others and sometimes give them the attention they seek. At times you will be gentle and yielding, at others hard, uncompromising, assertive, even violent. For the love that is born of sensitivity takes many unexpected forms, and it responds not to prefabricated guidelines and principles but to present, concrete reality. When you first experience this kind of sensitivity you are likely to experience terror. For all your defenses will be torn down, your dishonesty exposed, the protected walls around you burned.

Pluck Out the Eye

*And if your hand causes you to sin, cut it off; it is bet-
ter to enter life maimed than with two hands to go to
hell. . . . And if your eye causes you to sin, pluck it out; it is
better for you to enter the Kingdom of God with one eye
than with two eyes to be thrown into hell.*

— MARK 9:43ff.

When you deal with blind people it dawns on you that they are attuned to realities that you have no idea of. Their sensitivity to the world of touch and smell and taste and sound is such as to make the rest of us seem like dull clods. We pity persons who have lost their sight but rarely take into account the enrichment that their other senses offer them. It is a pity that those riches are bought as the heavy price of blindness, and it is quite conceivable that we could be as alive and finely attuned to the world as blind people are without the loss of our eyes. But it is not possible, not even conceivable, that you would ever awaken to the world of love unless you pluck out, chop off, those parts of your psychological being that are called Attachments.

If you refuse to do this you will miss the experience of love, you miss the only thing that gives meaning to human existence. For love is the passport to abiding joy and peace and freedom. There is only one thing that blocks out entry into that world and the name of that thing is Attachment. It is produced by the lusting eye that excites craving within the heart and by the grasping hand that reaches out to hold, possess and make one's own, and refuses to let go. It is this eye that must be gouged out, this hand that must be cut off if love is to be born. With those mutilated stumps for hands you can grasp nothing anymore. With those empty sockets for eyes you suddenly become sensitive to realities whose existence you have never suspected.

Now at last you can love. Till now all you had was a certain good-heartedness and benevolence, a sympathy and concern for others, which you mistakenly took for love but has as little in common with love as a flickering candle flame has with the light of the sun.

What is love? It is a sensitivity to every portion of reality within you and without, together with a wholehearted response to that reality. Sometimes you will embrace that reality, sometimes you will attack it, sometimes you will ignore it, and at others you will give it your fullest attention, but always you will respond not from need but from sensitivity.

And what is an attachment? A need, a clinging that blunts your sensitivity, a drug that clouds your perception. That is why as long as you have the slightest attachment for anything or any person, love cannot be born. For love is sensitivity, and sensitivity that is impaired even in the slightest degree is sensitivity destroyed. Just as the malfunctioning of one essential piece of a radar set distorts reception, and distorts your response to what you perceive.

Suffering and Glory

> Was it not necessary that the Christ should suffer these things and enter into His glory?   — LUKE 24:26

Think of some of the painful events in your life. For how many of them are you grateful today, because thanks to them you changed and grew? Here is a simple truth of life that most people never discover. Happy events make life delightful, but they do not lead to self-discovery and growth and freedom. That privilege is reserved to the things and persons and situations that cause us pain.

Every painful event contains in itself a seed of growth and liberation. In the light of this truth return to your life now and take a look at one or another of the events that you are not grateful for, and see if you can discover the potential for growth that they contain which you were unaware of and therefore failed to benefit from. Now think of some recent event that caused you pain, that produced negative feelings in you. Whoever or whatever caused those feelings was your teacher, because they revealed so much to you about yourself that you probably did not know. And they offered you an invitation and a challenge to self-understanding, self-discovery, and therefore to growth and life and freedom.

Try it out now, identify the negative feeling that this event aroused in you. Was it anxiety or insecurity, jealousy or anger or guilt? What does that emotion say to you about yourself, your values, your way of perceiving the world and life and above all your programming and conditioning? If you succeed in discovering this, you will drop some illusion you have clung to till now, or you will change a distorted perception or correct a false belief or learn to distance yourself from your suffering, as you realize that it was caused by your programming and not by reality; and you will suddenly find that you are full of gratitude for those negative feelings and to that person or event that caused them.

Now take this one step further. Look at everything that you think and feel and say and do that you do not like in yourself. Your negative emotions, your defects, your handicaps, your errors, your attachments and neuroses and hang-ups and, yes, even your sins. Can you see every one of them as a necessary part of your development, holding out a promise of growth and grace for you and others, that would never have been there except for this thing that you so disliked? And if you have caused pain and negative feelings to others, were you not at that moment a teacher to them, an instrument that offered them a seed

for self-discovery and growth? Can you persist in this observation, in your observation till you see all of this as a happy
fault, a necessary sin that brings so much good to you and to
the world?

If you can, your heart will be flooded with peace and gratitude and love and acceptance of every single thing. And you
will have discovered what people everywhere are searching for
and never find. Namely, the fountainhead of serenity and joy
that hides in every human heart.

Consider the Lilies

> *Therefore I tell you do not be anxious about your life....*
> *Look at the birds of the air.... Consider the lilies of the*
> *field...*   — MATTHEW 6:25ff.

Everyone at some time or the other experiences feelings of
what is known as insecurity. You feel insecure with the amount
of money you have in the bank or the amount of love you
are getting from your friend or the type of educational back-
ground you have had. Or you have insecurity feelings regarding
your health or your age or your physical appearance. If you
were asked the question, "What is it that makes you feel insecure?" you would almost certainly give the wrong answer.
You might say, "I don't have enough of the love of a friend,"
or "I don't have the kind of academic training that I need,"
or some such thing. In other words, you would point to some
outside condition, not realizing that insecurity feelings are not
generated by anything outside of you, but only by your emotional programming, by something you are telling yourself in
your head. If you change your program, your insecurity feelings would vanish in a second, even though everything in the
outside world remained exactly as it was before. One person
feels quite secure with practically no money in the bank; another feels insecure even though he has millions. It isn't the
amount of money but their programming that makes the dif-

ference. One person has no friends, yet feels perfectly secure in the love of people. Another feels insecure even in the most possessive and exclusive of relationships. Again the difference is in the programming.

If you wish to deal with your feelings of insecurity there are four facts that you must study well and understand. First, it is futile to ease your insecurity feelings by trying to change things outside of you. Your efforts may be successful, though mostly they are not. They may bring some relief, but the relief will be short-lived. So it is not worth the energy and time you spend in improving your physical appearance or making more money or getting further reassurances of love from your friends.

Second, this fact will lead you to tackle the problem where it really is, inside your head. Think of the people who in exactly the same condition that you find yourself in now would not feel the slightest insecurity. There are such people. Therefore the problem lies not with reality outside of you but with you, in your programming.

Third, you must understand that this programming of yours was picked up from insecure people who, when you were very young and impressionable, taught you by their behavior and their panic reactions that every time the outside world did not conform to a certain pattern, you must create an emotional turmoil within yourself called insecurity. And you must do everything in your power to rearrange the outside world — make more money, seek more reassurances, placate and please the people you have offended, etc., etc. — in order to make the insecurity feelings go away. The mere realization that you don't have to do this, that doing this really solves nothing, and that the emotional turmoil is caused solely by you and your culture — this realization alone distances you from the problem and brings considerable relief.

Fourth, whenever you are insecure about what may happen in the future, just remember this: In the past six months or one year you were so insecure about events which when they finally came you were able to handle somehow.

Lost and Found

He who finds his life will lose it, and he who loses his life
for my sake will find it. — MATTHEW 10:39

Has it ever struck you that those who most fear to die are the
ones who most fear to live? That in running away from death
we are running away from life?

Think of a man living in an attic, a little hole of a place with
no light and little ventilation. He fears to come down the stairs
because he has heard of people falling down stairs and breaking
their necks. He would never cross a street because he has heard
of thousands who have been run over on the streets. And of
course, if he cannot cross a street, how will he cross an ocean
or a continent or one world of ideas to another? This man clings
to his hole of an attic in the attempt to ward off death, and in
doing so he has simultaneously warded off life.

What is death? A loss, a disappearance, a letting go, a saying
goodbye. When you cling you refuse to let go, you refuse to say
goodbye, you resist death. And even though you may not realize
it, that is when you resist life too.

For life is on the move and you are stuck, life flows and
you have become stagnant, life is flexible and free and you are
rigid and frozen. Life carries all things away, and you crave for
stability and permanence.

So you fear life and you fear death because you cling. When
you cling to nothing, when you have no fear of losing anything,
then you are free to flow like the mountain stream that is always
fresh and sparkling and alive.

There are people who cannot bear the thought of losing a
relative or a friend; they prefer not to think of it. Or they dread
to challenge and lose a pet theory or ideology or belief. Or they
are convinced that they are never able to live without this or
that precious person, place or thing.

Do you want a way to measure the degree of your rigidity
and your deadness? Observe the amount of pain you experience
when you lose a cherished idea or person or thing. The pain and

the grief betray your clinging, do they not? Why is it you grieve so much at the death of a loved one or the loss of a friend? You never took the time to seriously consider that all things change and pass away and die.

So death and loss and separation take you by surprise. You choose to live in a little attic of your illusion pretending that things will never change, that things will always be the same. That is why when life bursts in to shatter your illusion you experience so much pain.

Be Ready

Therefore, you also must be ready; for the Son of Man is coming at an hour you do not expect.
— MATTHEW 24:44

Sooner or later there arises in every human heart the desire for holiness, spirituality, God, call it what you will. One hears mystics speak of a divinity all around them that is within our grasp, that would make our lives meaningful and beautiful and rich, if we could only discover it. People have some sort of a vague idea as to what this thing is and they read books and consult gurus in the attempt to find out what it is that they must do to gain this elusive thing called holiness or spirituality. They pick up all sorts of methods, techniques, spiritual exercises, formulas; then after years of fruitless striving they become discouraged and confused and wonder what went wrong. Mostly they blame themselves. If they had practiced their techniques more regularly, if they had been more fervent or more generous, they might have made it. But made what? They have no clear idea as to what exactly this holiness that they seek is, but they certainly know that their lives are still in a mess, they still become anxious and insecure and fearful, resentful and unforgiving, grasping and ambitious and manipulative of people. So once again they throw themselves with renewed vigor into the effort and labor that they think they need to attain their goal.

They have never stopped to consider this simple fact: Their efforts are going to get them nowhere. Their efforts will only make things worse, as things become worse when you use fire to put out fire. Effort does not lead to growth; effort, whatever the form it may take, whether it be willpower or habit or a technique or a spiritual exercise, does not lead to change. At best it leads to repression and a covering over of the root disease.

Effort may change the behavior but it does not change the person. Just think what kind of a mentality it betrays when you ask, "What must I do to get holiness?" Isn't it like asking, How much money must I spend to buy something? What sacrifice must I make? What discipline must I undertake? What meditation must I practice in order to get it? Think of a man who wants to win the love of a woman and attempts to improve his appearance or build his body or change his behavior and practice techniques to charm her.

You truly win the love of others not by the practice of techniques but by being a certain kind of person. And that is never achieved through effort and techniques. And so it is with spirituality and holiness. Not what you do is what brings it to you. This is not a commodity that one can buy or a prize that one can win. What matters is what you are, what you become.

Holiness is not an achievement; it is a grace. A grace called awareness, a grace called looking, observing, understanding. If you would only switch on the light of awareness and observe yourself and everything around you throughout the day, if you would see yourself reflected in the mirror of awareness the way you see your face reflected in a looking glass, that is, accurately, clearly, exactly as it is without the slightest distortion or addition, and if you observed this reflection without any judgment or condemnation, you would experience all sorts of marvelous changes coming about in you. Only you will not be in control of those changes, or be able to plan them in advance, or decide how and when they are to take place. It is this nonjudgmental awareness alone that heals and changes and makes one grow. But in its own way and at its own time.

What specifically are you to be aware of? Your reactions and your relationships. Each time you are in the presence of a person, any person, or with Nature or with any particular situation, you have all sorts of reactions, positive and negative. Study those reactions, observe what exactly they are and where they come from, without any sermonizing or guilt or even any desire, much less effort to change them. That is all that one needs for holiness to arise.

Will awareness bring you the holiness you so desire? Yes and no. The fact is you will never know. For true holiness, the type that is not achieved through techniques and efforts and repression, true holiness is completely unselfconscious. You wouldn't have the slightest awareness of its existence in you. Besides you will not care, for even the ambition to be holy will have dropped as you live from moment to moment a life made full and happy and transparent through awareness. It is enough for you to be watchful and awake. For in this state your eyes will see the Savior. Nothing else, but absolutely nothing else. Not security, not love, not belonging, not beauty, not power, not holiness — nothing else will matter anymore.

More series books on the next page

Modern Spiritual Masters Series

Simone Weil
Writings Selected with an Introduction by
Eric O. Springsted
ISBN 1-57075-204-4

"The penetrating vision of Simone Weil pierces our self-
deceptions in this wise, well-edited selection from her late,
most important works. A unique and unforgettable spiritual
guide in what promises to be an important series."
—*Sally Cunneen*

Charles de Foucauld
Writings Selected with an Introduction by
Robert Ellsberg
ISBN 1-57075-244-3

"If ever we needed to hear the prophetic voice of Charles
de Foucauld, it is now in our days of selfishness and
confusion. His unfettered path to God is a marvel of holiness
and pragmatism. His unfettered path to God is a marvel
of holiness and pragmatism. Here is the fine introduction
to his approach and thought that will lead many others
to take Brother Charles into their hearts and lives."
—*Paul Wilkes*

Please support your local bookstore, or call 1-800-258-5838.

For a free catalogue, please write us at
Orbis Books, Box 308
Maryknoll NY 10545-0308
or visit our website at www.orbisbooks.com

Thank you for reading *Anthony de Mello.*
We hope you enjoyed it.